BEAUTY BEHIND BATTLES

"DISCOVERING YOUR PURPOSE THROUGH THE DARKEST MOMENTS, STORMS AND HARDEST TRIALS OF LIFE"

By

Mih Bibiana M Dighambong

TABLE OF CONTENTS

PRAISE FOR
"BEAUTY BEHIND BATTLES"

"I have been blown away by the rawness and honesty that emanates from Mihzuh Bibian's profound words. Her dedication to her faith and religion, despite the hardships she has faced in her life, has inspired me greatly and given me the confidence to know I can rise above all that life has thrown at me."

- Joyce Evans

"Bibian's book encapsulates the power of the human spirit and displays how God's glory shines through us. It shows us that despite great suffering and sacrifice, there is redemption and a chance at a victorious, fulfilling life. Bibian's emphasis on self-love and self- discovery is greatly appreciated and illustrated in this book, as we find that the best way to live a full life is through great belief in ourselves."

- Lisa Smith

"Mihzuh Bibian writes with such poetic grace. Her writings in her latest book "Beauty Behind Battles" are one that touches not only the heart but also the soul, with its deep understanding of the self and of our Lord's plans. In reading her words, I was urged to reflect on my own spirituality and my own journey. Nameseko's story is one painted with suffering and pain but also with such joy and elegance. It teaches the value of truth and of faith."

- Robert Tenu

"In her Book Beauty Behind Battles, Mihzuh Bibian speaks from her heart as a woman of faith and a visionary leader. She provides a much-needed dose of hope, A timeless beacon of hope and light in our dark world; though we see ruins, behind those ruins lies true beauty, blessings and light. It's brightness beyond

4

the battle. The horizon can be overwhelmed with the fog of fear and the haze of regret, but victory is on the other side of what looks like defeat. It's a universal masterpiece that cuts across all cultures and societies- with God, it is rarely what it seems, but faith at work. It elucidates the moment we feel we cannot go on for one more minute and cry out to God for the strength to keep going! Reading the lines in this book, I was amazed to know that there is glory beyond the battle! To trust His voice even through the unknown because That is where miracles are birthed!"

- Lucille Elinor

"At an age where our world has lost its moral compass, Bibian's book serves as a mirror for ourselves. Beauty Behind Battles impassions every human pains and afflictions. It is an encouraging, uplifting, and powerful work- A clarion call to create a more just, sustainable world. Even in our struggles and deepest darkness, we can all make our world safer, fairer, and healthier for all humanity...."

- Nkurunziza Hakizimana

DEDICATION

This Book is dedicated to all who have suffered Abuse, Social Injustice, Violence, and the Wounds have crippled them from accomplishing their Dreams. The Message in this book is Your Healing balm- A JOURNEY TO RISE ABOVE ANY SITUATION OR TRIALS, UNLEASH YOUR GOD GIVEN POTENTIALS, TURN YOUR PAIN INTO PURPOSE AND BECOME ALL THAT GOD CREATED YOU TO BE!

YOU ARE CREATED FOR BLESSING!

FOREWORD

December seven years ago, at the exit door of the sacristy of the University Parish of the Archdiocese of Yaounde, Cameroon, Bibiana approached me saying: "Thanks for the homily, Father! Anyone who is not disturbed by the ongoing crisis in Anglophone Cameroon is not human. People, especially women, girls and children are suffering" she said, as tears ran down her eyes like a river. The tears were a language communicating experienced and/or witnessed traumatic events whose memories had been triggered by the homily of the day. There began our journey of spiritual companionship, a healing journey of wounds, and a journey of compassion and empathy for humanity.

Her book entitled "BEAUTY BEHIND BATTLES".

"DISCOVERING YOUR PURPOSE THROUGH THE DARKEST MOMENTS, STORMS AND HARDEST TRIALS OF LIFE" is a third-person narrative about a fictive but universal character by the name of 'Nameseko' (God's gift), an attractive but questionable name. Like Nameseko, a good number of us have had our childhood, adolescence, and adulthood intertwined by obstacles, pains trials and suffering. The gender of the character is symbolic and representative of the most fragile and vulnerable persons in our communities who are exposed to higher risks of victimization and multiple forms of gender-based violence (GBV).

Nameseko's trust in God is at the center of her resilience. She believes that; "When the world appears to be crumbling, don't lose hope, for Christ Jesus in you, is the hope of glory" (Col. 1:27). The narrator's voice, accompanied by some mental health tips for processing grief, loss, and trauma are a milestone towards sensitizing those who might walk through the same path like her in their life's journey. Albeit being the fruit of your memories, experiences, relationships, and beliefs, you can, however, always forge an identity. Identity formation has to do with discovering and developing your potential, choosing your purpose in life, and finding opportunities to exercise them. Nameseko developed a strong sense of identity that permitted her to understand, appreciate, and express her unique perspective, participate actively in the community, and contribute positively to societal change.

This is not just a book but it is all our shared life's experiences as humans lived out to discover and harnessed through life's struggles and adversity, the seeds of GOD's richest potentials buried inside each one of us.

Who you are versus who you would like to be may be conflicting. However, reading these lines will inspire you to forge your identity and purpose.

Dr Laisin Frankline

Community Psychologist

PREFACE

This is a fictional narrative. The central character Nnamseko is a fictional character who x-rays our societal ills in order to heal our fallen humanity. The characters, events or experiences in this book are not related or connected to any individual/s or groups of person.

This is not just a book but it is our stories. It is our collective experiences as pilgrims in a journey called life-The university of Tears. No one is exempted from pains or trials. Our lives are interconnected; we're meant to learn from one another's experiences. We can all benefit from each other's stories.

It does not depend on your race, position, statues, white or black, rich or poor, Life's battles, twists are part of our human existence. This is a practical hand book that teaches us how to respond to lifes trials and tribulations of any kind. The book urges us not to let our pains be in vain.

As we learn to surrender and trust in the power of our Creator, He fills our emptiness and voids with resilience, New Hope and Vision to use our stories in Serving, Building, Shaping a Better World for all Humanity.

CHAPTER ONE-

PROLOGUE

She sat on the veranda with a book in her left hand and a crucifix on the right. Her heart was very heavy, her eyes began to faint, and she grew weary and tired. She could not understand why things were happening this way. Many things began to cross her mind, and she asked herself, "What is the meaning and purpose of life?" Impossible for her to get a satisfactory answer to her question at the moment, she opened a page in the book she was holding.

Despite the tears in her eyes, she managed to read a few lines: "The pains, trials, tribulations, and temptations that we face are inflicted upon us by satan and/or self. When God, in his wisdom, allows adversities in our lives, we should never believe the falsehood that the discipline of the Lord is proof that he has rejected us. Rather, it is evidence that we are his sons and daughters, if indeed, we are. It is entirely possible that the sufferings we endure are a direct result of our commitment to Christ."

At first, she could not grasp any meaning out of these lines since her present pain was too severe and her past full of hurt. She, however, continued asking some rhetorical questions in relation to the choice and significance of her name. Why do people call me Nameseko? Why did my parent choose this name for me? Was it not a mockery of my personality? How was I a gift from God? She reminded herself of the many sad experiences she had gone through and concluded that she could never be a gift from God but rather a curse and bearer of bad news. She was determined to change her name.

Nameseko was in her late 30s. This feeling in her was groomed based on the premise that she was growing old and had achieved

very little or no success in life. All of life to her was but misery and pain that left her with scars from a horrible past.

Nameseko was born at a time when her mother was at the height of crisis. When her mother shared her crisis experience with her, she felt more confused and asked why she could not be named "Problem child" instead of God's gift. The response of the mother was that she would come to understand when she grew older. Indeed, this was the mystery that preoccupied Nameseko's mind and she was yet to understand the real meaning of it.

One glorious day, Nameseko was reading the Bible, and her eyes caught a verse in the book of Ruth 1:20-21 that reads: "And she said unto them, call me not Naomi, call me Mara; for the almighty hath dealt very bitterly with me I went out full, and the Lord hath brought me home again empty; why then call ye me Naomi, seeing the Lord hath testified against me, and the almighty hath afflicted me?" Touched by the content, she grew interested in reading what women had written in the Bible. She then moved on to the writings of some prominent feminine writers and began thinking.

Was Naomi's reason for changing her name the same as Nameseko's? She was a collection of tragedies. She had weathered many storms. At her age, she was very discouraged with life. Discouragement comes when people think they have experienced all sorts of bitterness in life. But no matter one's age, no one can experience all in life. There are no graduations from the school of life other than death.

No one knows how God will end his book, but he does turn to save the best for the last; maybe this was the only consolation she had for holding the Bible. Though she was still crying, she managed to finish reading the book of Ruth. By the time she finished reading the book of Ruth, she felt a deep relief and said to herself: "Never allow changing times to change who you are. It is dangerous to lose your identity in circumstances surrounding you.

Circumstances can change, and when they do, one may feel empty and unfulfilled." This is what happened to Naomi in the Bible. She added that, in spite of her bout of depression, God still had a purpose for her to fulfill in life. So, just because life's challenges are high doesn't mean your life has come to an end.

With this, Nameseko became confident, as if she was conversing with someone. She remarked: "If you feel that yours has come to an end, you need to redefine your purpose, gather your assets, and keep on living and giving. As long as you can maintain a sense of worth, you can resist the "Mara mentality." But how could she resist that when all that came from within her spoke of nothing else but agony and anguish? She heard an internal voice telling her: "Trust in God, and somehow, through someone, some time, and somewhere, God will reconnect with your stumbling soul. Suddenly, a door will open, and you will not feel abandoned anymore. That is real salvation." The voice was very eminent and loud. She felt a presence but could not differentiate if it was real or just an illusion.

Nonetheless, it existed right beside her, just like a companion. She started becoming aware of that presence, especially when she felt lonely and distressed. It comforted her during her painful moments when she had no one to share with. As she carried on, another voice from within told her: "Pay keen attention to the positive ideas, moods, emotions, impulses, memories, and beliefs that are constantly coming to your consciousness. Whatever stimulates your sense of aliveness could be a message from God or the very presence of God within you." The message was very powerful. She turned to see if someone was talking to her, but all was still and quiet. The voice became louder, and she sank into the world of dreams. The loud voice, which could still be heard, was now conflicting with the turmoil she had. Then, out of a sudden, peace descended like a shower of blessings; she had fallen into a deep sleep.

There was peace everywhere. She saw beauty and life and ran out for it, but the more she ran after it, the more it moved away from her. She couldn't get hold of it. She struggled and stumbled. It was quite painful because she had some difficulties to move through. She felt as if her legs and hands were tied. She cried out for help. She shouted at the top of her voice, but no one could hear her. She could only hear echoes. She felt the weight of her legs lessen and resumed walking but could only stagger since she was getting tired. She stopped and saw a beautiful garden in front of her. It was a beautifully cultivated garden, varied in form and color. The garden was full of trees bearing fruits of all kinds. Colorful flowers blossoming, the freshness and radiance of the landscape on a May morning becoming strong in her mind.

She saw on the other side of the garden, a beautiful city. The whole city appeared sparking, with striking features exposed to the sky like ships' towers, domes, temples, and a gracefully flowing river. It was a sight to marvel at. At first, she was struck by the splendor and gorgeous nature, but then the houses merged to form a magnificent tower. How she was to get there was her major worry. She heard a voice from within her; "Move on, don't be frightened or discouraged; you shall be right there" She didn't know where she got her courage from. She kept moving on, sweating and breathing like one from a fruitless venture. But hers was a goal she was about to grasp.

As the thought of giving up came to her mind, she felt someone stretch out a hand to her; at first, she was reluctant to grasp it. When she finally gave in, she felt some extra energy and consolation. The hand walked her into the beautiful city.

She could not believe what she saw. "This is Paradise," she said to herself. She noticed that a wild landscape in a fertile valley's free-ranging growth can reveal God. Everything was scented with peace and tranquility. The calmness and gentleness of the surroundings were enough to reveal to her the presence of God in all things. The natural beauty, the rustling of leaves in the trees, the fast-flowing streams, the vast expanse of the ocean, and the rolling green hills brought a sense of relief to her broken heart. She felt highly lifted, and she smiled in total amazement.

A weary mind or a tense body can feel its life return by contacting nature. In her state, she felt she was transformed into a higher level of existence. She felt elevated, and a kind of peace she had never felt before surrounded her at the moment. The atmosphere itself bore a sense of lasting joy and happy moods, stillness, and quiet moments. "This is what it means to live," she told herself. "I wish to live and die here," she continued. "But where are the people who live here?" she asked. She got the answers but sensed a feeling of extreme joy and security alone in nature. She kept telling herself that she belonged here and that she was not going back to the world of noise and pain. She was now enjoying the wonderful melody, a lyrical splendor from birds and animals that gave joy to the ear and heart. She thought she had found out what she was looking for- a way of finally escaping from everything that so distressed her in the complicated, fragile, and dark world. She decided to make this place her home so as to remain in contact with every aspect of the surroundings.

As her thoughts and imaginations went from one beautiful scenario to another, and her joy of existing in such a peaceful environment grew, her journey to the dream world was interrupted by a loud argument in the neighborhood that woke her up. "Was this just a dream?" She exclaimed. She surveyed her surroundings and it was different. Where had she been? What was happening to her? The book and the crucifix she had in her hands were lying somewhere away from her. She regretted the fact that her experiences were just a nightmare. She sensed that she was now in the world where she actually belonged: a world of pain and suffering.

It was almost 6 pm, and she was lying on the veranda. The children were not yet back from their evening lectures. She wanted to meet someone to share her dream with, though she did not cherish nor believe in dreams. Years back, she had dreamt that her younger brother died, and a few days later, her dream came true. However, this one was different. She had this dream at a time when she was getting frustrated, almost wanting to give up everything because she had been through the worst times and her future was bleak. The events of her life had made her become helpless and defenseless. She felt like a crumbling rose. Her problems didn't begin suddenly. They had existed ever since she was born and had tainted many areas of her life.

From her experience, she learned to trust in God totally. Given the fact that her trials were quite challenging, this created an emotional handicap, leading to dependency at different levels. Relationships can become crutches. An affected person can place such weight on people that it strains a healthy relationship. If you are becoming increasingly dependent upon anyone other than God to create a sense of wholeness in your life, then you are abusing your relationship. Wholeness cannot come to a desperate person rummaging through other people's lives. One of the things that a hurting person needs to do is to break the habit of using other people as a narcotic to numb the dull aching of an inner void. The more you meditate on the symptoms or rehearse the problem, the less chance you have of allowing God to heal you.

Nameseko had all these lessons to learn from all that had befallen her in life. Yes, she was on a trip called life. She didn't choose the tour, neither did she buy the ticket. All that she had experienced was the cost of what she paid for the happiness she had chosen. Life is like a toll road. This she admitted, knowing one is on an adventure. Life is a pilgrimage, a trip to and a tour through a land you've never traveled before. You made a decision one day to embark on the path, not knowing the price.

Yes, the price you have to pay might seem high, but recall all the pleasures, satisfactions, benefits, and rebirth of positive possibility thinking. Your heart will move from pain to praise. Pay the toll and thank God for the trip you've had. Nameseko did just that as she recalled her lots in life.

It was getting dark, and she had to prepare the evening meal, but the thought of her worries made her reluctant and hesitant to do anything. She loved cooking and doing house chores. Her mother had owned a restaurant, she had every reason to be an expert cook. She had taught Nameseko how to make many special dishes. For so many years now, she had used her expertise in her home. Though her husband never approved of her as a good cook, the encouragement she had each time friends and guests tasted her food made her confident.

But why was she reluctant to cook today? She had felt so terrible on this particular day. This was one of the worst days of her life. She had had an argument with her husband. Had she not run away, it would have resulted in a fight. By the time he was leaving, he had promised hell when he came back. Full of fear, she had no courage to cook for that day. Nameseko spent most of her days in tears, and this made her forget herself most often. She simply accepted her role as defined for her by her husband. She seldom had a good conversation with him. In fact, she was happy when he spent days or hours outside of the house. "But what would he say if he comes home today and his meal is not being served?" she wondered with fear. He will accuse her of laziness, remind her about her church activities, and say that she was good for nothing.

Though sometimes she had stopped her daily hours of worship because it was becoming an area of problem in her marriage, she prayed silently. "Oh God, please give Sean a sign to make him love and respect me. As you can see, dear God, I am in real pain." Then she started to think again. She felt there was too much to explain, too much about herself that she did not know. There was this particular ache in her heart, too heavy for tears, too heavy for words. There was no time to wallow in self-pity.

She had had so many things bottled up inside her. Life with Sean, her husband, was purgatorial. She began to realize that she was not living with the husband of her dreams but an enemy. How he had treated her all through her difficult times not only gave her a sense of emptiness but a picture that was too horrible to print. She felt hollow and didn't feel highs or lows anymore. At times, she wished she could get into a minor car accident and end up in the hospital. She didn't want to die; She just wanted a rest from him. Despite these thoughts, the husband had more reasons to criticize her and tear her down.

She dreamed about leaving, but he constantly told her no man would ever want a broken, lonely, thinly fleshed single mom, and she believed him. He promised he would fight her with his fists and all his power if she ever thought of leaving. Sean was capable of this because he was quite an influential personality in the community. That's one thing about intimate partner violence (IPV). It happens slowly; one cut at a time to one's self-esteem until they start believing their abuser and the little voice that is their conscience dims.

At about 10 pm, she heard a sound at the gate; sure her husband was returning. The children had all gone to sleep. Though she felt frightened and was panicking, she told herself to be strong. She began praying again and again within her, asking God to save her from subsequent beatings. All the same, considering that the torture and stress were part of her day-to-day life, she began to think that either God was tired of answering her prayers or he wanted to teach Nameseko a lesson.

Before Nameseko even went to open the door, he was shouting at the top of his lungs. Nameseko sensed danger. As she went closer, she saw the terrible anger on his face. It was a sad indication. She wanted to say welcome but kept quiet. The sharpness of his voice seemed to remind her: "I am the man in charge, and when I talk, you don't talk. I dowried and married you, and not the contrary. You are my property, and I will treat you the way I want." She would have loved to protest this but remembered her mother had told her never to argue with a man when he was just coming home. It could be he was running from trouble, had an argument with friends, or was simply drunk. But her husband was not good at drinking. He took just enough for himself.

In her confusion, she managed to let him in, but the frown on his face worried her. She was about to heat the food and serve him when he ordered her to come.

"Where have you been? Where did you go to? To church because that is the only thing you are good at?" She did not know which of the questions to answer first; she simply kept quiet. "Answer me, you idiot," he went on. "Or do you want me to squeeze saliva out of your mouth?" Nameseko began to feel scared as he looked at her with a wildness in his eyes. "Someone saw you in town today. What did you go to buy this time?" She wanted to say she hadn't left the house since morning, but he simply stopped her; "When I am talking, you don't talk; I don't want to listen to your lies"

Now, with what type of water was Nameseko to wash herself clean of these dirty accusations? How was she to tell Sean, while he was in such fury, that she had not left this spot since morning? She had simply been contemplating her woes. She looked up to heaven, gathered courage, and told him softly, "Sean, wouldn't you come in and have a rest, take your meals, then we can settle down to talk? Was this the reason why we got married?"

The word marriage drove him mad. "Did you say marry?" he retorted angrily. "Married to who? You are a burden, and your presence is hell to me." She did not understand this growing animosity of her husband towards her. He glanced at the phone in her hands. "Give me the phone!" Who called you today? How many people have you called today?" She chose to keep quiet because whatever answer she would have given would not have brought any calm. She left and walked to the room. He followed her into the room. "This is rudeness. So this is what you have learned; to walk out on me. Today you will leave my house and go to meet those training you to be heady to me. I am sick and tired of a woman who cannot take simple instructions"

Nameseko wanted to ask if she was his slave, just taking instructions. What can one say to such a man? That he is an idiot? That he is selfish? That he is a perpetrator? Nothing Nameseko could think of could convey her feelings at that moment adequately. She simply sighed and sat on the bed. He tried to pull her up, but she resisted, her heart pumping between her ribs.

It was now getting confrontational. She had done everything to avoid it getting to this level, but there were many factors working against her. She was weak and naïve. Sean took this as an advantage of her. At an impulse, he bounced on her, dragged her up and down in the room. She felt slaps all over her body, struggled to run out, but the door was cruelly slammed. The slamming of the door reminded her of a past experience. He continued with the beatings till she was covered with bleedings, trembling and crying bitterly. A recollection of her entire woes ran through her mind at that moment as she felt abandoned, rejected, and beaten like an animal. She began to lose control of herself. In her bitter thoughts, she felt the weight of the world on her shoulders. There was no mother, father, or relative to come to her rescue, except her children.

What do you do when you are trapped in a transitory state, neither in nor out? When you're left lying at the door, torn up and disturbed, trembling and intimidated? What do you do when you don't know what to do? When you're filled with regrets, pains, nightmare experiences, and can't find relief. Nameseko could only cry the more. Her heart ached as her mind went through her disasters, calamities, and woes. Was the world not too full of sadness? All the torments and bitter experiences clouded her memories. Every bitter pill she had tested in life was recreated and painted in her subconscious. The shock of all the bad times, horrible experiences, and the heaviness she was feeling at that moment drove her crazy.

Why was the world so cruel? Why was she born? Why did God choose such an existence for her? Were the burdens not too severe for her to bear? Was the current of life not too severe and hard on her? The lots, the loads she was carrying, made her physically weak and gave her the kind of attitude that made her feel she was a carrier of pain. She lamented to her God, "God, where did I go wrong? Please, God, tell me, why must I go through all these things?" At the mention of God, she felt angered. She was angry with God for allowing all that happened in her life. All these were shaping her life, but she did not know. "If you won't take me, my God, then give me strength to live through this, help me to overcome, give me another life for my children's sake" was all the prayer she could remember to tell God.

Though she had stopped crying, her heart remained heavy and bitter. Suddenly, she heard a voice within her: "Have courage for the great sorrows of life and patience for the small ones. When you have laboriously accomplished your daily task, go to sleep in peace. God is awake. There is a light in this world, a healing spirit more powerful than any darkness we may encounter. We sometimes lose sight of this force when there is suffering and too much pain. Then suddenly, the spirit emerges through the lives of ordinary people who hear our cry and answer in extraordinary ways."

What was left for her in the world? What had she not seen? On every mark of trouble, she found her name written on it.

In fact, from Nameseko's look, you could easily see that she had been a patient all her life, not from any physical disease but as a result of the bitter waters she had drunk out of life. Like a crumbling rose, she had suffered as a result of the long-range aftereffects of a painful past.

Memories of her sad childhood experience, lack of fatherly care, love, and protection, rejection and abandonment, growing hatred, conflict, and envy amongst her relatives, and an abusive, unhealthy, and unhappy marital life could only increase her grief. From her woes, calamities, and tragedies, she began to agree with Thomas Hardy (1886) that happiness is but an occasional episode in the general drama of pain and suffering.

Despite this conception of life, Nameseko had total trust in God. She believed and held on to the fact that despite all odds, raging storms, and blows we received from life; it will still take the authority of God's word to put the past under our feet. It is important to remember that for every person, there will be a problem. But most importantly, for every problem, God has a prescription! With all these thoughts in her, she painted a picture of her life as she recalled every event and scene with the following scriptural verses to guide her: "Blessed is the man that walks not in the counsel of the ungodly, nor stands in the way of the sinners, or join those who have no use for God. Instead, they find joy in obeying the law of the lord, and they study it day and night. They are like trees that grow beside a stream, that bear fruit at the right time, and whose leaves do not dry up. They succeed in everything they do" (Psalm 11:3). "Where no counsel is, the people fall: but in the multitude of counselors there is safety" (Proverbs 11:14).

CHAPTER TWO-

HIDDEN WOUNDS FROM CHILD ABUSE AND NEGLECT

If someone must be hurt, if it ever becomes necessary to bear pains, weather strong winds, or withstand trials and opposition, let it be an adult and not a child. It is important to note that most adult problems we are fighting to correct are often rooted in the ashes of difficult childhood experiences. Every time you see an insecure, vulnerable, intimidated adult who has unnatural fear, low self-esteem, or an apologetic posture, there is every indication they are a survivor of child abuse.

Nameseko's thoughts went back to those childhood memories. Each person who has been through these adversities has their own story; so does Nameseko. She had had some degree of cracking, submitting to the ineffective narcotics of a sinful and perverted lifestyle, falling prey to snares. The fact that she persevered is a testimony to all who understand what it means to be abused as a child. Broken homes often produce broken children. Poor children are often caught in the crossfire between angry parents. Like many children, Nameseko was wounded by the unfriendly atmosphere between her parents.

It is easy to be thoughtless and cruel. One might be walking along a path and happen to notice one flower with a bent stem. Perhaps a bird had landed upon it, and the stem had given way under the weight. But careless people do not concern themselves with the causes and backgrounds of brokenness, and so they slap off the delicate blossom and toss it aside. When a candle wick bums down and begins to flicker and shoulder, even though it is yet able to give a little light, we almost instinctively blow it out.

After all, it is no longer what we need. It has become less important and less effective than it was meant to be. Nameseko carried an unpleasant aroma of bitterness from the tragedies of her early days. The story her mother told her illustrates her feelings. When she was about eight years old and they were living in the village, her mother could not afford money to make her a birth certificate. She told her the whole story:

"It all began like a dream. My dream was to get married one day and bear children for my husband. I lived with my mother since I was the eldest and being a girl, my parent never allowed me to go to school. Instead, my mother was happy keeping me by her side. I took care of my junior ones, and eventually, when they grew up, they were sent to school."

Nameseko became curious about the story. "So, you never went to school because you were caring for your junior ones?" Nameseko asked.

The mother replied, "Yes, sometimes during farming seasons, when my mother slept in the farm, I stayed with them. Because of this, my parents could never think of sending me to school. When I was fifteen, many suitors came asking for my hand in marriage. I chose your father amongst the many. Besides the fact that he was handsome, average, tall, and fair in complexion, he was coming from the coast. At that time, it was a pride for any woman to be married to someone from the coast. No further thought was given than to accept his hand in marriage. This turned out to be a baptism of fire.

The traditional marriage "knock door" was done. It was a very poor one. He brought three tins of oil, a jug of wine, and a few bottles of beer. My people were very discouraged but accepted the gift reluctantly; they felt that he was going to make up as soon as the children started coming, but they were just dreaming because they were yet to discover they were just dancing on broken bottles. This was the saddest day of my life. I soon discovered that your father only wanted a show up. He was not prepared nor serious about it. He came late, drunk, and left early without even the proper marital rites. His brother represented him towards the end."

Mama started sobbing. Nameseko asked, trying to wipe her eyes; "Mama, why are you crying?"

"It's so painful my daughter," She said. "I wish it never happened."

"What?" Nameseko inquired.

Mama continued her story:

"Three months later, I discovered I was pregnant when your father had left. It was always the case with the so-called people from the coast. They hardly spent time in the village. They gave one excuse and the other. You will hear them say, "My leave expired yesterday, so I must go." When I discovered it, I felt disgruntled and disappointed. I was pregnant with a stranger I called my husband. I had hardly settled down to know whether he loved me or not, and now my virginity was destroyed. I wept and begged God to do something. I wrote to him but no response came. When I was in the 8th month of the pregnancy, he sent some items with the baby's needs in mind. I was happy, though I still felt he should have come to take me rather than allow me to give birth in our compound. I could not bear the shame and disgrace. I finally gave birth to a male child. With all hopes and respect, I knew he would be happy with the news. I thought, at least this will make him excited to come and take us. It was normal for any man to bring up his children and not allow other people the responsibility to do so for him. But where was your father? No word came; his uncle came with palm wine and some cola nuts. This was in recognition that the child was theirs. I wanted to send them away, but my mother stopped me. My mother explained to me that according to tradition, when you give birth in your father's compound, you cannot leave until the baby has been weaned, and this must be after two years and above. This was hell to me. My mother earmarked that this could be the reason for his not coming, but to me, he was simply wicked and taking cover under a careless and ruthless traditional custom.

When he finally came, he brought gifts for everyone in my family. I did not want to see nor talk to him, but with the child, what was I going to do with him? Friends advised me to forgive and accept him for the sake of the child. After giving it a second thought, I reluctantly accepted, hoping that he would do the traditional cleansing by reimbursing what was spent on the child for all the years. That he did but promised that he would come to take us in a month's time.

Within this period, I discovered I was pregnant. I thought informing him would make him hasten up, but it worsened the situation. He never came until I gave birth to you. It was such a painful experience for me. I don't wish to recall it. It was in the midst of this darkness, pain, and desolation that you were born."

Nameseko could not help herself, so she started crying, but her mother held her closely and continued.

"Your father never showed up. I became an object of mockery to my sisters and family members, a laughing stock to my friends. I had been a good and obedient girl all my life, never wanting to give my body to anyone unless it were to someone I would call my husband. I had never thought of disgracing my parents. Though from a poor family, I promised to make my parent and younger ones proud.

I knew I was to set a very good example by getting married and living with my husband for my younger ones to emulate.

I became frustrated, disgraced, and abandoned. The men who had wanted to marry me and whom I refused took the story far.

My sisters, who initially sympathized with me, started calling me names and insulting me. I became a burden to my poor parents. And I was with two kids. My parents could no longer bear taking care of me and the children. I felt the world on my shoulders. Without asking anybody's opinion, I hatched a plan in my heart. Two years was too far a period to wait again. I decided to carry the two of you to meet your father. You were such a beauty and charm; in spite of everything, everybody admired and adored you.

I knew that if your father saw you, his carbon footprint, he would not hesitate to accept us, but my expectations were a nightmare as I received the shock of my life. I took the night transport and a friend helped and took me to your father's home. With two children and luggage, I was too tired and exhausted. All I needed was to see a house where I could put both of you and rest."

My mother's eyes began to water as she continued her story. "As we knocked, it was a young lady with two little children who came and opened the door. At first, the friend thought we were at the wrong place but your father suddenly showed up, looking like a fierce and wounded animal. He asked what I was doing in his house, and he did not bother to turn his eyes on you and your brother. I did not need a soothsayer to tell me what was going on. Not knowing what to say in the midst of all the confusion, I carried both of you out of the house and out of your father's sight. It was fifteen years later that your father could know if he ever had children somewhere."

Mama ended her stories with both of us sobbing heavily. It was with bitterness, heaviness, and feelings of rejection and abandonment that Nameseko recalled and printed those memories in her mind's eye. She told herself, "So Mama went through all these horrible years alone?" Yes, she admired her courage and determination. She saw in her mother some extraordinary strength. She had singlehandedly taken care of her kids and gave them all that needed two people or more to give. In all, she was proud of her mother.

However, memories of what her mother had gone through made Nameseko promise in her heart that she was going to make her proud. She closed her eyes and wept bitterly. It was an unthinkable malice for her father to throw away his own children. She could not understand why people could be so cruel and irresponsible, even towards their own offspring.

In spite of all her questions, she could not arrive at an answer. She imagined what could have happened if she, at one point, thought of transferring her pain and anger toward the kids.

Nameseko crowned her mother her queen of everything. The mystery of her entire life and the grace Jesus has given her stood revealed. It dawned on her that God never abandons but will always watch over his own in times of great need and desperation. Nameseko could afford to look back in the crucible of trials as from within and without, her soul was refined. She raised her load like a flower after a storm and saw how the words of the psalmist had been fulfilled in her case- The Lord is my shepherd, and I shall want nothing. He makes me lie in pastures green and pleasant; He hath led me gently beside the waters; he hath led my soul without fatigue .... Yea, though I should go down into the valley of the shadow of death, I will fear no evil, for thou, o Lord art with me (Ps 22:1-4).

CHAPTER THREE-

WOUNDS FROM ADVERSITY: A VICTIM OF ANIMOSITY

In her childhood, Nameseko experienced hatred from friends and family members. It was never because she did something wrong to anyone but entourage made her feel like an outcast. The hate wound can be one of the most soulcrushing, devastating, and life-altering cycles in our lives and relationships. The experiences Nameseko felt had taken roots from her childhood and adolescence. She lived with many relatives who did not really love her or accept her for who she was.

Namseko grew up in a dysfunctional, chaotic, and addicted family. This was the reason why she often felt inadequate, defective, or broken, and these feelings did not magically disappear. These feelings of inadequacy stocked in her, plaguing her into adulthood. This was what she had to endure, being raised in a dysfunctional family with a lack of self-worth. Children in dysfunctional families often experience some form of childhood trauma due to physical or emotional abuse, neglect, abandonment, witnessing violence, homelessness, etc... She identified herself with a list of experiences common amongst children in dysfunctional families.

Nnamseko was overtly told she was bad, difficult, stupid, ugly, inadequate, unlovable, and the cause of the family's problems by the relatives. She was blamed, yelled at, called derogatory names, and criticized harshly. Even if she wasn't told directly, she surmised that she was the cause of her family's problems because there was no other explanation given for her outright rejection as a child. Her guardians did not pay enough attention to her feelings or emotional needs. They didn't notice when she was sad or upset. They didn't comfort her or ask her what was troubling her. She experienced what was called Childhood Emotional Neglect (CEN) or emotional abandonment.

In fact, she was abandoned and hated. Her father physically left her for all her life, and she was estranged from him for the rest of her life. The relatives she grew up with didn't tell her they loved her or show her any affection. Most often, she was abused physically, sexually, and emotionally because of neglect. She had to act like a parent and grow up too fast. Her parents or caregivers didn't keep her safe.

Even though her parents never physically hurt her, they created an unsafe environment through their addiction and mental illness. Especially her mother, with her failure to supervise her, drunkenness, domestic violence, angry tirades, and allowing unsafe people into the home. She lived all her life in fear and had to walk on eggshells, trying to keep everyone happy to prevent anger and abuse.

All of these experiences made her believe that there was something wrong with her, that she was so bad and flawed that even their parents could not love her. Being ignored, invalidated, and rejected causes us to feel ashamed. And shame is built on the belief that you are deeply and fundamentally flawed. To live with shame is to feel alienated and defeated, never quite good enough to belong. It is an isolating experience that makes us think we are completely alone and unique in our belief that we are unlovable. Secretly, we feel like we are to blame. Any and all deficiency lies within ourselves.

You probably came to believe that you caused your parents to reject or hurt you. This was the only explanation that made sense when Nameseko was little, and it was the only way for her to survive. Children need adults to survive. Even very dysfunctional or abusive parents provide some of the basic necessities, like food and shelter, for their children. So, we were wired to attach to our parents, to be loyal to them, to want to please them so we can survive until we get mature enough to take care of ourselves.

The truth is that her parent's dysfunction and problems made them incapable of caring for her and loving her the way all children deserve to be cared for and loved. As she grew into adulthood, she realized that her parent's deficiencies were not her fault, but as a child, it was safer to believe so. As a result, the belief that she was inadequate or unlovable got embedded in her belief system. Namseko felt a sense of shame thinking about all the negative and unhealthy experiences. It kept her from talking about what had happened to her family, so these beliefs festered and grew.

Like many who have lived through rejection, she felt worthy by becoming a perfectionist and people-pleaser. Since she doubted her own value, she was always seeking external validation. She needed others to tell her and reassure her that she mattered, that she was needed. Over the years, she came to the understanding that this pattern never created selfworth because there's literally nothing that anyone can say or do that will change how we feel about ourselves except us. Building self-worth and healing childhood trauma is a process. Sometimes, it can seem overwhelming because there are multiple layers of pain and distorted beliefs, but it's possible to develop an internal sense of worth and adequacy by making small, consistent changes.

The hurt of rejection usually arises when a child feels like they are arousing disinterest or indifference – which may be real or simply felt! Equally, empty and indifferent gazes, insensitive words, sighs of exasperation, busy and unbothered parents, the feeling of being too different. Sometimes, it doesn't take much to create this feeling of rejection in the child, and it can intensify with recurrence. Sadly, this was all that occupied Nameseko's mind and thoughts. The feeling of rejection can also come from being loved for reasons other than who we truly are. This gives the impression that who we are holds little value for others. Also, it can create doubt in our minds about being truly loved or lovable.

Nameseko felt most often like a child used by a parent to cause pain to the other during separation for their own personal gains. She was aware of why she was being rejected, but she ended up believing that she was worthless and without interest! Over time, this feeling turned into selfdeprecation, which turned into a sense of emptiness. This emptiness became an endless quest for love and belonging, as well as a major source of anxiety and panic. The perception of rejection, whether false or exaggerated, risks causing a child to frequently reject themselves – to leave the ship before it sinks! This is an attitude that aims to protect them emotionally, which also denotes a form of shame and self-loathing. This self-loathing can also arise when the child experiences guilt. However, guilt is more typical of the wound of humiliation, where the child has the feeling of being incorrect or ridiculous to the point of adopting selfpunishing and masochistic behaviors. Rejection and humiliation can sometimes intertwine. Rejection has to do with the "being," while humiliation touches on the "doing."

All of these truths, Nameseko learnt later in life, after her childhood was tainted.

Loneliness, Flight, and Self-Sabotage

The fear of rejection leads the child to make himself/herself small and go unnoticed. This may lead to daydreaming and building a fantasy world to live in, as well as loneliness, even in the presence of others. She/he might also erect walls of protection around themselves that may become their fortress of solitude, which may greatly affect their social development. Indeed, this loneliness can lead the child to want to keep to themselves: who they are, what they could have to offer, or what they would be able to create, just like an oyster that wants to remain closed and keep its pearl, mistakenly thinking that no one wants it. That might create an inkling to withdraw from others to avoid feeling uninteresting while blaming others for that disinterest. It is a form of projection and unconscious self-sabotage mechanism.

Without realizing it, the child will often create favorable conditions for their own rejection. This is what a recent psychological theory on peer rejection proposes. However, on the vibratory and energetic level, this is already selfevident. This is because what we feel, we vibrate, and we create that feeling in matter; we attract it. Also, the child who feels rejected tends to avoid groups and generally has few friends. All relationships may seem precarious in their eyes, making them constantly fearful of losing their relationships and ready to fall back into their shell at any time!

Adolescence; Sensitive Times

Since the personality is in construction, adolescence is certainly a sensitive period. The body experiences hormonal surges and changes. One of them, dopamine, stimulates new experiences and social connections. Consequently, the hurt of rejection can be greatly exacerbated during this period. Among other things, it can make the rejected person more sensitive to teasing. Also, the need for belonging becomes more insistent, sometimes even to the detriment of selfesteem and personal boundaries.

Anorexia, for example, is often motivated by a need to please but which expresses a form of self-rejection, a desire to escape or disappear. The person rejects food like one rejects love from others. Bulimia, on the other hand, also motivated by a need to please, expresses a sense of shame towards one's body. It is fed by the masochistic mechanism (deprivation, indulgence, guilt, and self-punishment) specific to this wound.

Consequently, the desire to please, the attraction for bonding with friends, the vagaries of romantic experiments, and insufficient emotional maturity are all elements that can turn the knife in the wound, particularly that of rejection, where the person can come to thicken the walls of their fortress of solitude.

Fear of Commitment and Relationship Losses

Due to the self-sabotaging attitude and persistent fear of rejection, commitment can be difficult for adolescents. In addition, the fear of not being able to create new connections makes it very difficult for them to lose a relationship. This often leads to a miserable or depressed state. For children, this can be their imaginary world, video games, etc. In adults, it can be work, successive relationships, drugs, alcohol, etc.

In fact, each type of wound has difficulty experiencing this loss, but not for the same reasons and does not cause the same reactions. For the wounds of betrayal and injustice, the loss will cause more of a combat reaction. In wounds of betrayal, loyalty is at stake, and aggression will be used to control the other. For injustice, the wound is the feeling of not deserving what is happening, and aggression will be used to punish the other.

For the wounds of abandonment and humiliation, the reaction will be more akin to helplessness and vulnerability. For abandonment, the feeling of being alone and without a safety net will cause "victimhood" and self-pity. For humiliation, it is the feeling of not having done enough for the relationship, generating shame and guilt.

At a young age, the hurt of rejection, humiliation, and injustice can be very similar – the common link between them is the fear of not being loved and a marked attitude of dissatisfaction with oneself, with words like "nothing," "suck," "weak," and "stupid." If it relates to "doing," and the child seems to experience frustration and seek perfection by using words like "I must..." and "I should..." ... and being demanding of himself or others, it is more about injustice. When these words are expressed with concern, and the individual seems to fear being criticized, punished, or made to feel guilty, it is more about humiliation. If the concern seems to be WHO he is as a person and wants to

33

shut down, sulk, and flee uncomfortable situations, it likely pertains to rejection. Nameseko had this wound of rejection all over her; this wound of rejection lived in her for so long.

It has often been said that the antidote to any emotional difficulty is to allow ourselves to embrace our emotions. Embracing our emotions means feeling, understanding, verbalizing, and getting rid of them. What makes those emotions such a burden is that they remain unexpressed and/or unappeased. This creates a cumulative effect that impacts our perception of reality and, consequently, our beliefs and behaviors—a kind of mental programming!

And so… How do we, as parents, allow children to embrace their emotions? By leading the way, by allowing ourselves to embrace our own emotions, to be vulnerable, imperfect, and human. By doing this, our children will learn to feel safe doing the same. Thus, they will know that they will not be judged, rejected, or punished if they do. On the contrary, they will be welcomed, comforted, and loved.

Going to The Heart of the Wound

The older we get, the more mental and emotional protective mechanisms there are. They serve to protect us from the original trauma. When we have intense emotional reactions, the mind tries to limit the damage. First, it tried to make us forget the pain that we may have felt. Then it programmed beliefs and behaviors to prevent this from ever happening again.

Unfortunately, this also prevents the integration of the experienced trauma. This emotion is then kept in a vibratory form somewhere within us… until it can be felt again, understood, and released. That liberation brings about a new understanding which can then render obsolete the beliefs and protective behaviors put in place to this day.

Of course, this approach may seem counterintuitive to the mind … And you don't deprogram your brain overnight! That is usually done in successive stages or steps, depending on what the person is ready to release, understand, and integrate at that time.

Therefore, feeling your emotions requires good preparation to calm down and develop the capacity to observe yourself in the present moment… Meditation is certainly great for that! It also requires an attitude of non-resistance to let the emotion rise. The less you resist, the faster you get it out!

Reconnecting with Yourself

The key to any healing process is to reconnect with yourself. This greatly facilitates being more self-accepting and forgiving, more attentive to our needs, and recognizing our value. We cannot change the past, but we can give ourselves what we have waited in vain from others. Learning to take care of yourself may take time and a lot of love; things you have to learn to give yourself. So be good and patient with yourselves.

The wisest, most loving, and well-rounded people you have ever met are likely those who have been shattered by heartbreak. Yes, life creates the greatest humans by breaking them first. Their destruction into pieces allows them to be fine-tuned and reconstructed into a masterpiece. Truly, it's the painstaking journey of falling apart and coming back together that fills their hearts and minds with a level of compassion, understanding, and deep, loving wisdom that can't possibly be acquired or attained.

We come from all sorts of backgrounds, cultures, social and economic positions, sets of beliefs, religious affiliations, values, and morals. They are all based on how and where we have been raised. We call this our "family of origin." Family is defined as 'the significant caretakers and siblings that a person grows up with, or the first social group a person belongs to...often a person's biological or adoptive family.'

We can tell stories about how we were raised. We all can and do. And often, we hear friends say, "I'm never going to make the same mistakes my mom or dad made." Yet many times, they live out these very same patterns in their own lives because these bents toward certain habits, reactions, and mistakes get passed down from generation to generation.

Some are good, and some are not so good. Some can even be categorized as curses.

Generational patterns play significant roles in how we view ourselves and how we view God and others. Our sense of belonging and identity normally comes from our childhood development within our families. From them, we learn who we are as individuals. Unfortunately, though, some have battled significant wounds from their youth that have caused them to believe the lie that they are unworthy, unvalued, unaccepted, and unloved. And because of this many unconsciously or even consciously reject themselves. Why? Because the rejection caused by external circumstances pierced their very souls and became part of their emotional make-up.

A wounded heart can then become numb and hardened against the world, God, and the individuals closest to it. Of course, there are many forms and layers of rejection and different types of wounds. Some cause people to lash out when triggered by something said or by an unpleasant event in the external environment. When, how, and why are they triggered? And what triggers the negative reaction?

When we perceive a threat, it becomes our reality at that moment, and we go into a flight, fight, or freeze mode to protect the core of our being, our heart, from being crushed one more time. This method of coping seems to lessen the perception of rejection, woundedness, and pain. We don't want to admit that we are being reactionary, yet our reactions—even our facial expressions—give away our secret. We are wounded individuals in need of healing.

Have you felt this type of rejection or woundedness and then reacted in a vain attempt to protect your heart? Nameseko had it countless times. After experiencing the shock of rejection all her life, she needed more than simply the ability to cope with it. All she actually needed or wanted was to belong, to feel loved, and to be loved unconditionally.

She told herself, there is hope! There is an answer! And that is to be found in our Savior - Jesus. If rejection is part of your story, try to recall who or what rejected you and how it first happened. Then, realize that Jesus knows and understands rejection. It says so in Isaiah 53:3-5 that He was wounded and rejected by many people. Jesus wants us to give these wounds over to him, receive his unconditional love, and then be totally healed. I know - this can sound trite, possibly even like a cliché. But it's true!

Then, during the healing process, these painfully deep inner wounds can appear to threaten us as they are being exposed and brought to light. But it is so worth it to receive the coming and full healing. And there is a tremendous benefit for future generations in our family. Behind every amazing woman is a story of blood, sweat, and tears. In front of that woman is a testimony that God is about to write through her trials, where fire and pain turned into glory and triumph.

Namseko found these strategies helpful for increasing her self-worth and decreasing feelings of shame:

- She grieved for what she didn't get as a child.

- She practiced self-compassion, especially compassion for the part or parts of her that felt unworthy or unacceptable.

- Acknowledged her feelings; because they matter.

- Challenged negative thoughts and beliefs about herself. Asked herself questions such as: How do I know this thought is true? Where did this belief about myself come from? Is there another, more helpful way to think about myself or this situation? Is this my thought/belief, or is this something I was told as a child?

- She chose to believe good things about herself. She said positive things to herself, and when others said nice things about her, she believed them.

- Also, she worked a lot with a therapist and attended a support group. Both can be very helpful in reducing shame.

CHAPTER FOUR-

THE GREATEST WOUNDS: ABANDONMENT AND LONELINESS

Nameseko went through an intense emotional crisis of abandonment that created a severe trauma hard enough to leave an emotional imprint on her psychobiological functioning, affecting her future choices and responses to rejection, loss, or disconnection. Following her abandonment experience as a child through adulthood, she developed a sequel of post-traumatic symptoms, which had sufficient features with post-traumatic stress disorder. This was considered a subtype of her diagnostic category as she suffered silently with this over the years. As with other types of post-trauma, the symptoms of post-traumatic stress disorder of abandonment range from mild to severe.

Post-traumatic Stress Disorder (PTSD) of abandonment is a psychobiological condition in which earlier separation traumas interfere with current life. An earmark of this interference is intrusive anxiety, which often manifests as a pervasive feeling of insecurity – a primary source of selfsabotage in our primary relationships and in achieving longrange goals. Another earmark is a tendency to compulsively reenact our abandonment scenarios through repetitive patterns, i.e., abandoholism – being attracted to the unavailable.

Another factor of abandonment post-trauma is for victims to be plagued with diminished self-esteem and heightened vulnerability within social contexts, including the workplace, which intensifies their need to bolster their flagging ego strength with defense mechanisms that can be automatically discharged and whose intention is to protect the narcissistically injured self from further rejection, criticism, or abandonment. These habituated defenses are often maladaptive to their purpose in that they can create emotional tension and jeopardize our emotional connections.

As a Victim of abandonment trauma, Nameseko had emotional flashbacks that flooded her with feelings ranging from mild anxiety to intense panic in response to triggers that she was never conscious of. Once her abandonment fear was triggered, it led to what Daniel Goleman (1995) calls emotional hijacking. During her emotional hijacking, the emotional brain took over, leaving her feeling a complete loss of control over her own life, at least momentarily.

As the emotional hijacking occurred, the chronic emotional excesses led to self-depreciation and isolation within her relationships, as well as giving rise to secondary conditions such as chronic depression, anxiety, obsessive thinking, negative narcissism, and addiction. This was all deposited inside Nameseko.

Post-traumatic stress disorder (PTSD) is a so-called "disease" of the amygdala – the emotional center of the brain responsible for initiating the Fight Flee Freeze response. With PTSD, the amygdala is set on overdrive to keep us in a perpetual state of hyper-vigilance -action-ready to declare a state of emergency should it perceive any threat even vaguely reminiscent of the original trauma. The amygdala, acting as the brain's warning system, is constantly working to protect and overprotect us from any possibility of further injury. In the post-trauma sequelae related specifically to abandonment, the amygdala scans the environment for potential threats to our attachments or our sense of self- worth.

Nameseko suffered from PTSD, from abandonment, which heightened her emotional responses to abandonment triggers. This was often considered insignificant by others. For instance, depending on the circumstances, when she felt slighted, criticized, or excluded, it instigated an emotional hijacking, interfered with her, and even jeopardized her personal and professional life.

The shock occurs partly because whenever she felt deserted or cheated on, it usually came as a final blow in a mind-numbing, repetitive cycle of emotional abuse. Elusive abuses of her self-esteem weighed her down over time until she came to accept it as normal. Only when you are on the receiving end of the final blow does the manipulation, undermining, and devaluation you have been living with sink in.

Emotional abuse comes in many flavors. It is actually a form of brainwashing that can rapidly undermine your quality of life. Other forms of abuse, such as yelling, criticizing, bullying, etc., are also easy enough to recognize. However, covert psychological abuse is difficult to detect and substantiate. It eats away at your self-esteem and can cause you to question your sanity before you know it.

Nameseko had lived through this, and it flew in her brain and ran in her veins. She had openly questioned her very existence because of what she had drunk and lived through.

Emotional wounds can be even more devastating than obvious blows to the physical body and can have much longer-term effects. These hidden injuries pose a grave threat, not just to our physical but also to our emotional or psychological well-being.

A physical blow is understandable to the mind. When someone hits you, at least you can identify the source of the pain. But, when you are psychologically abused, you are hurt and do not feel safe, yet cannot comprehend why. The longer it goes on, the more likely you are to obsess about the situation, to feel unhinged, and to lose your confidence and trust in yourself and your perceptions.

Psychological abuse is virtually impossible to prove. Emotional abusers have an impressive arsenal of tools for subtle psychological control and torment. Nameseko's abuses were unending stressors ranging from constant putdowns and criticism to subtler tactics, such as deception, manipulation, withdrawal, invalidating, stonewalling, triangulating, threats to leave, revising history, or refusal ever to be pleased. A steady stream of these corrosive insults undermined her sense of self until she questioned her reality.

We all engage in some of these behaviors when we feel especially powerless or frightened. But for some people, these defenses are more a way of life than a reaction to unusual life stresses. If you are involved with an abuser, he or she is likely highly focused on control. They routinely alternate warmth and affection with withdrawal or insults to keep you in line. Should you question their tactics or threaten to leave, they will pull out all the stops to draw you back in. This was Nameseko's life. Often, they turn the tables to accuse you of precisely what they are doing to you, casting themselves as the victim of your unbearable behavior to justify their actions. Since we naturally blame ourselves when we feel disoriented or are in pain, the finger-pointing adds fuel to the fire of deteriorating self-confidence.

If you have been deceived, abandoned, or betrayed in an intimate relationship, acknowledging the emotional abuse involved is central to understanding what has happened and recovering. By unilaterally leaving or betraying you, the person you likely trusted most in the world has inflicted a life-changing, destructive blow to your well-being.

As sudden as the shock of discovering their deceit or unfaithfulness may be, your undermining has probably been going on for some time. You likely have been living in an atmosphere of deception and manipulation. Mixed messages of caring and contempt have already short-circuited your neural wiring with conflicting yet urgent approaches and avoid signals toward your partner.

When the final blow is administered, the trauma leaves you shattered and dazed, unsure of who you are or who you were in a relationship with. To your traumatized mind, your former partner becomes both your executioner and your potential savior from the bewildering pain. The depth and elusiveness of the invisible emotional wounds make them difficult to recognize and understand and equally difficult to heal.

When you learn your supposed loving partner or spouse, to whom you have devoted your life, is not at all loving or devoted to you, it is a shock. For some of us, the pain sets off a spiritual and existential crisis. Having your trust shattered by the person you counted on most to be there for you questions your very understanding of human nature, of good and evil. If you have been through the soul wreckage of betrayal, you know how difficult it is for anyone who has not to believe what it can do to a person.

Waking to the deception you have been living releases a kind of "time-release poison" into your system that infects all your memories. Without conscious intention, the brain must slowly, painfully revise each memory associated with the relationship to fit the actual facts. The entire context of your past needs rewiring. Even years later, a new memory may be triggered and take you down.

If you are like Nameseko, you will feel vaguely ill, bewildered, as well as enraged and despairing while this adjustment goes on. Each memory that surfaced exploded like a little time bomb that sent shock waves through her body and wrenched her heart. She went for a massage, sweet self-love deep within her soul that left her so full of warmth and affection flooded into her memory. Still, the memory was too saturated with the realization that, at the time, she needed to heal, in order to deal with the cumulative emotional blows that overwhelmed her life-Another tragic event will resurface injuring her existing wounds.

The temptation was huge to avoid these torments. Various addictions and distractions lured her to avoid the somatic distress of dying in her imagined past. As the difficult truth sunk in over and over again, it is important not to make the mistake of glossing over the damage by telling herself it is no big deal. Her crisis of faith in the goodness of life was real.

There is a reason the betrayal of an intimate attachment has been called "the most difficult of all wounding," "the most deviant form of attack," "a wound beyond words," "an irreparable devaluation," the most underrated traumatic experience," as well as "the greatest evil."

Nameseko found it difficult to be gentle and patient with herself as she went through this ordeal that took years. She kept thinking it shouldn't have taken so long. She was fortunate to have a lot of help to ride out the shock waves and to learn to patiently take care of herself like she would a sick child.

In recovering from abandonment or betrayal, learning about destructive narcissism can help you heal. Naming this brand of emotional abuse opens the door to denial of the facts of what has happened. What a relief for Namseke to realize she was not losing her mind. Nor was she alone in this unhinging experience. It was not all her fault, after all.

It gave her back the ground to learn such charming yet disordered personalities exist. Those who learned to survive by undermining and shaming others. These people pulled her in with charm and attention, then began to devalue, ignore, insult, and often discard her.

She hardly saw it while she was caught in this web of gratification and hurt pleasure and fear. The slow-drip confusion and pain of emotional abuse breeds denial for selfprotection. Also, the covert abuse, laced as it is with warmth and affection, kept pulling her back in. The hot, cold, unpredictable behavior kept her in constant unease, anxious and insecure. Yet, she longed for crumbs of warmth and affection from them to soothe her jangled nerves.

Living through narcissism, she began to understand how easily a biochemical "trauma bond" forms in these circumstances. How notoriously difficult these bonds of pain mixed with pleasure are to break. Most importantly, she saw that she would need help to recover. This is why learning about narcissism in betrayal recovery was vitally important to her healing. Eventually, in coming back from the dark hole of lost trust, she needed to move beyond focusing on the abuse. Otherwise, it would have become a barrier to her heart opening that truly needed healing. To recover from the soul loss and to restore trust in life and ourselves, we need the vast healing capacities of the heart.

Recognizing what happened to her helped her come out of the protective haze of denial to face the broken heart. *Dropping into the heart opened the door for her towards compassion* but at a price. Moving into the heart means feeling the pain of what had happened. While this movement cannot be rushed, there, in the midst of her own brokenness, she made a startling discovery. There, waiting for her to find holiness and love as loving spiritual forces appeared ready to help, hold, and heal her deep wounds.

Brokenness does not feel like a place where holiness would want to dwell. Yet, as she fell into the grief of betrayal, she bathed bit by bit in the warm outpourings of tenderness. Then, something even more surprising happened. She began to sense in her bones the suffering of the one who hurt her. As she softened, she saw the bewildered, shamed, angry little one behind his manipulative, hurtful armor. Compassion flew as a miracle, freeing her heart from the heaviness of harm.

The term "victim" has become a dirty word in some circles. Should someone claim they have been injured or victimized in a relationship, especially if their wounds are not physical, they are met with shaking heads or raised eyebrows.

Nameseko could not tell how many times, when she was reeling in shock, she was advised, often with the best intentions, to "stop being a victim!" This was because she had acted like one for all her life. When she discovered she had been living a lie, it injured her. It undermined her reality, shattered her trust, and stirred depths of pain incomprehensible to her at the time. She needed compassion and understanding more than ever before in her life.

She was often accused of not taking responsibility for her part in the relationship's demise, suspected of wallowing in a "poor me" mindset, and charged with character assassination for suggesting she had been harmed. But, above all, she was chastised for taking satisfaction in taking on a new and exciting identity as a victim!

These life facts are being severely blended in Nameseko's upbringing and her entire life, though she often fought hard to keep her painful memories away from her. Despite the pains and trauma, she did not want to accept the position the world had given her. She was quietly reminded, "There is no such thing as a victim." Or "Nothing can hurt us but our own attitudes." She was highly susceptible to believing these attitudes because, for most of her life, she, too, felt disdain for victims. She believed she was a psychologically sophisticated person who understood that she was responsible for her own feelings. And spiritually "advanced" enough to believe she "attracted her reality." She told herself this most often: "Previously, I had considered myself a resilient person who bounced back with relative ease from life's slings and arrows. I believed others could do the same if they just put their minds to it".

Despite her refusal to believe in her ordeal and the devastating impact it had on her, she often looked back with so much pain, disgust, and hate. She understood what her thoughts could lead her to and its repercussions on the future of her loved ones. She exclaimed in total despair, "Until this traumatic abandonment and betrayal fractured my world. Then, despite all my efforts to heal, to let go, and to forgive, I did feel like a victim. For a long time, I could not share the feeling of shame at having been "used and abused" in short, victimized. Somehow, this unrelenting pain must have been my fault."

It happened that with the passage of time, she wanted to take a stand for victimization. She had come to believe that in order to move forward and heal, there are moments we need to stand up and shout: "Yes, I am a victim! But this does not define my final identity! Yes, I am a victor!"

Nameseko began to wonder why we are so anxious to blame victims. To be a victim implies helplessness and acute vulnerability. By denying victim status to those who are hurt in life, we attempt to banish our own fears of harmful events. We can see how absurd the belief in "no victim" is. It concerns natural disasters, war, genocide, rape, epidemics, and children abandoned or born into poverty or abusive families. Yet, we still tend to rationalize misfortune when it is close to us, blaming the victim for their plight, even if we clothe our blame in concepts such as sin, karma, or the law of attraction.

We like to believe we live in a predictable world, a safe and moral universe where our actions have consequences. If only we lived, thought, and acted well, terrible things wouldn't happen to us. "What goes around comes around" gives us a sense that we have some control over our destiny. That misfortune is random and can happen to anyone at any time is terrifying. But the truth is that bad things do happen to good people. When we blame the victim, it offers us a last grasp of control. If they had behaved differently (like us), this bad thing would not have happened to them.

At the deepest spiritual levels, there may be some truth that the victim of abuse, accident, disease, or crime shares responsibility for their suffering. From the human perspective, however, when we are faced with suffering, these attitudes not only cover fear of our own powerlessness but shut off our sense of compassion.

When life deals with either us or someone we love, it shatters naive innocence and trust. Moreover, if this blow comes through the hands of another we have loved and trusted, we are forced to grapple with questions of good and evil.

Betrayal initiates an existential, spiritual crisis that requires spiritual healing. Namseko had to dig deep inside and dispel many illusions to find answers. She had passed through the dark night of realizing how much she did not know. Most importantly, she needed to find her way to a trusted superpower beyond human relationships. When a traumatic event shatters our reality, we need to come to terms with what happened against the titanic draw of denial. This includes our victimhood, helplessness, and powerlessness. Until we do this, we cannot fully grieve our loss and reach acceptance, thus healing.

Nameseko learned that acknowledging "I am a victim" can be a statement of profound courage, compassion, and insight. To move forward, first, we need to stand on the firm ground of what happened. We need to face the existential crisis the truth initiates. Then, we can find our way to the compassion and strength that goes beyond victimhood. This solid strength endures regardless of what happens to us. Like Llewellyn Vaughan-Lee (1997) says, "Our heart knows what our mind has forgotten - it knows the sacred that is within all that exists, and through a depth of feeling, we can once again experience this connection, this belonging."

Nameseko gave herself credit for living with a broken heart. A broken heart testifies that she had taken the first steps on a pilgrimage to a deeper and more compassionate life. To be touched to the quick by losing her love, she had taken the risk of caring. She had opened her heart to cherish, trust, and depend on something higher. Opening one's heart in an intimate relationship goes against the grain of our protective shells; it takes guts. We must find the courage to trust that much before we can love. . . and before our heart can break. When we open up to love, whether we realize it or not, we are agreeing to be deepened and changed by the alchemy of loving. Often, that change comes about in ways we cannot anticipate.

A broken heart is one of those ways. The loving heart has to break, it seems, in little everyday disappointments or with one big blow to grow into a more complex, tender intimacy with ourselves, life, and our humanity. When loving brings betrayal or loss, if we can find the patience and grace to bear gently with the disintegration of our world, love's alchemy intensifies its paradoxical work. It marinates you in a rage, fear, loneliness, grief, and despair you can barely endure. But when we are cracked open and fall into the scary depths, fragmented pieces of the heart nourish our dark places and magnetize the healing light of the Holy Spirit within. In the dark times, as invisible hands school us in kindness towards our brokenness, love wounds gradually transform. Compassion, strength, and wisdom take root in the loamy ache we thought would never end.

For Nameseko, this developed an exquisite sensitivity to the suffering of others. One day, as if by a miracle, she woke up to find her heart had grown into a fresh new sensuality and love for this confusing, beautiful life. Throughout the long months and years of grieving over Sean's total neglect and abandonment, she gradually reframed loving so deeply as an act of bravery and faith, not naïveté and delusion, as she originally believed. Yet, trusting enough to love him, though he proved to be a faithless partner, was the first step in awakening to a more vibrant faith in her heart's lush, compassionate mystery.

CHAPTER FIVE-

DEALING WITH CUMULATIVE LOSS AND GRIEF

We are told to move on or "just get over it" and fast. But unattended grief leads to long-term suffering. This was the experience of Nameseko. If you've been traumatized or have experienced deep grief after the death of a loved one, a breakup, a divorce, or a betrayal, you know you don't just move on. Pain isn't something to "just get over." And you never, ever forget; Nameseko did not. Dealing with the loss of many close family members and dealing with some personal serious illnesses made Nameseko lose the desire to move on. Nameseko's experience of grief teaches us how to live with pain, navigate loss, and grow.

Within thirteen years Nameseko recorded multiple losses, with no time to recover in between. In March 1996, she lost her elder brother, who was everything to her; this was when she was preparing for her end-of-course examination in High School. In April 2001, she lost her mum due to complications from traumatic failures "My Mum meant the world to me; she was my world." Losing her at her prime without ever testing the fruits of her labor brought Nameseko to the point of total confusion, frustration, and depression. The life plan that Namseke had in mind for herself didn't include the loss of her beloved mother, her best friend.

Even as she took care of her in the hospital for weeks, she believed in her heart that her mother would get better; she was torn between the hope that all would get better and the reality that continued to decline. When she died, she felt pains she had never experienced. As the days turned into weeks and the weeks into months and years of agony, Nameseko's pain did not seem to relent. She felt as if she had lost her world, her mind, and her faith. Nameseko's grief was consuming, and she could not find comfort.

Her junior brother passed away from sudden death in 2003. (He was only 18 years old). A few months later, she lost her brother-in-law, and barely two months her father passed away after a brief illness. Two weeks later, Nameseko became severely dehydrated and was admitted in the hospital, during which time she suffered a stroke, which left her unable to use her left side and affected her memory. She underwent inpatient rehabilitation for months to try to regain function. She continued to rehab in her home and then as an outpatient. As she was trying to heal, she lost her aunt and grandmum in 2009.

No one around her could fully comprehend her woes and tragedies. It was too heavy and severe. Many thought she was going to die from the many shocks and tragedies. She, at one moment, believed she was meant for the grave. Many times in her sleep, she dreamt she was in the grave amongst the dead. In her mind and heart, she felt nothing but sorrow. Nameseko developed a sciatic nerve that extended to severe back pain. Her case was brought to an orthopedic physical therapist, where she shared an uptick in caregiver health issues and was taken care of by a caregiver.

In essence, the neurologist shared that her body had the ability to disregard feeling pain while taking care of others – a version of disenfranchised grief. This made sense, and Nameseko felt a sense of relief. She kept pondering on how to take care of her frail and weary body; compartmentalizing grief did finally catch up with her. Was her body now telling her she had to deal with everything she was keeping bottled up to stay strong for her loved ones?

In the summer of 2011, she was diagnosed with a serious advanced nervous condition, for which she was successfully treated with a lot of physiotherapy and psychotherapy. She was able to return to work too soon, mostly because she needed to live a normal life. During her treatment, her only exposure to the outside world was with members of her church group. Worship and prayers became her way of life. Her reality at that time was that it was normal to go through her ordeal.

Why was this happening to her? Did she really have time to grieve since all these things happened one after the next? As she pondered over all these, she felt so depressed. In her desperation, she cried, "I don't want to go on. I can't drive because of my stroke; everyone has left me. I am stuck in my pain and feel like a prisoner; I can't walk outside with a walker, which fatigues me so much. I'm not sure it's worth it... I wonder if anyone in this life has had to deal with multiple issues quickly."

"To change, people need to become aware of their sensations and how their bodies interact with the world around them. Physical self-awareness is the first step in releasing the tyranny of the past." (Bessel A. van der Kolk, 2014). While the ideal way to cope with different types of grief is to express the emotions that come with bereavement, it's common to avoid the emotions and suppress grief from showing its true colors. Nameseko did not know this.

When someone encounters one loss after another, unaddressed grief can compound into what's known as cumulative grief or cumulative losses. It's overwhelming and challenging, and it can feel as though life is crumbling to pieces in every direction. Cumulative grief is something that can accumulate over the years or even decades and seriously affect your physical and mental health. There's no timetable for how long someone can grieve a loss, and if they never address the loss of a loved one, they walk around with suppressed emotions bottled up, waiting to be released. This is exactly what Nameseko had been going through without knowing.

Nameseko's story is similar to many. The loss of a loved one is one of the most difficult trials we can face in life. Understanding what grief is and what it is common for people to feel when someone dies can help us experience a measure of peace while grieving. Grief is the emotional and often physical response we have when we experience loss. The more profound the loss, the more profound the grief will be. Grief can involve virtually every emotion or can leave us feeling numb and disconnected from the world around us.

Manifestations of grief may include hopelessness, anxiety, anger, denial, guilt, incapacitating fatigue, difficulty in controlling emotions, lack of concentration, loss of interest in people or activities, and feelings of being overwhelmed. Nameseko was an embodiment of all these symptoms.

Sometimes, the hardest part about grief is simply not understanding what is happening. Knowing a few principles can help us successfully navigate our own journey through grief. Though grief is painful, do not avoid it. Grief hurts, but when allowed to do its work appropriately, it can be the salve that helps us heal. The first step in handling grief is to recognize that the pain is a normal part of the process. It needs to be acknowledged, not avoided.

In times of grief and lamentation, many, like Nameseko, question their faith in God. Nevertheless, the promise from Isaiah 53:4) is reassuring: "Surely he hath borne our griefs, and carried our sorrows." The scriptures are filled with examples of grief, loss, and the associated pain. Job grieved deeply upon learning of the death of all his children (Job 1:18–21; 2:13; 6:1–3). After a tremendous battle between the Nephites and Lamanites, thousands were slain, and "surely this was a sorrowful day; yea, a time of solemnity, and a time of much fasting and prayer." Although David's son Absalom caused him great disappointment and sorrow, David loved him deeply, and the scriptures are clear about the pain he felt upon learning of his son's death (2 Samuel

19:1-4). Grieving is not a brief process. Be patient with it and give it time. As with a physical wound, the pain of losing a loved one requires time to heal.

To express sorrow as one grieves is not a mark of lack of faith. Many good people wondered if they had lost faith because they felt profound sorrow at the passing of a loved one. They mistakenly thought that a person with a strong testimony should not feel deeply saddened at a loved one's passing away, as if mourning the loved one's death were synonymous with disbelief in the afterlife or the Savior's promise.

With the shortest verse of the Bible, "Jesus Wept!" John 11:35 shows Christ's profound grief over the loss of his friend Lazarus, and this did not equate to loss of faith.

There is a price we pay for loving someone. The Savior has said, "Thou shalt live together in love, in so much that thou shalt weep for the loss of them that die." I have come to learn that grief is the price we pay for loving someone and that the price is worth it. No one can say they would give up the love they had for a family member in order to avoid the grief that came from losing them. When loved ones pass from one side of the veil to the other, they continue to be just as important to us as when they were with us. Because we love them, we can't really expect to completely "get over" losing them.

If we have ever stood at the bedsides of many people who have passed from this life, these countless experiences should strengthen our knowledge that our loved ones are in many ways as present with us after death as they are during life. We cannot typically see them, but they are often there to help us through our various challenges, including our grief over their passing. "Sometimes the veil between this life and the life beyond becomes very thin. Our loved ones who have passed on are not far from us." This was what Nameseko gradually came to realize during her long years of pain, grief, and tragedy.

It is equally important to note that grief opens to atonement. Death is part of our existence here on earth. Nevertheless, through the atonement and resurrection of His Son, our heavenly Father has provided a way for us to overcome death and be comforted and healed. Through the power of the atonement, "the sting of death" can be replaced by the peace that the Spirit brings.

Just as the lame man at the pool of Bethesda needed someone stronger than himself to be healed, so are we dependent on the miracles of Christ's atonement of our souls to be made whole from grief, sorrow, and sin. Death's sting is softened as Jesus bears the believers' grief and comforts them through the Holy Spirit. Broken hearts are mended through Christ, and peace replaces anxiety and sorrow. Referring to the sorrowful Friday on which Jesus's followers grieved His death and then to the glorious Sunday on which He was resurrected, each of us will have our own Fridays. Nonetheless, I testify to you in the name of the One who conquered death that in the darkness of our sorrow, no matter our desperation, no matter our grief, Sunday will come. Some nights are much longer than others, but the morning always follows.

Death brings deep sorrow, but our joy will exceed our ability to comprehend when our reunion with deceased loved ones finally comes. Yet peace is not reserved for the next life only; we can feel peace now, even in the very moment we are feeling pain. How thankful we can be for the sacrifice of our Savior and the healing power His atonement can bring us in spite of our grief. "Weeping may endure for a night, but joy cometh in the morning" (Psalm 30:5).

In her hours of prayers and meditation during the long periods of her grief, Nameseko reflected, "Our Heavenly Father ... knows that we learn and grow and become stronger as we face and survive the trials through which we must pass. We know that there are times when we will experience heartbreaking sorrow, when we will grieve, and when we may be tested to our limits. However, such difficulties allow us to change for the better, to rebuild our lives in the way our Heavenly Father teaches us, and to become something different from what we were, better than we were, more understanding than we were, more empathetic than we were, with stronger testimonies than we had before."

CHAPTER SIX-

FINDING HOPE IN THE DARKNESS OF GRIEF

The only way out of pain is through pain. No one teaches us how to use pain in a positive way. We don't know how we can learn from the challenging aspects of life to grow as individuals. During trial, you learn healthy ways to cope and move forward. You learn how to put yourself into a safe space to admit your grief and start attending to it. We cannot heal what we don't feel. Grief demands to be felt, and when you decide to address it in a healthy way and in a safe space, you save yourself the turmoil of the grief creeping up on you when you least suspect it and when you need to be functional to get a task done. We must name it and be with it. Not forgetting it but integrating the loss into our emotional states in a healthy way.

Nameseko knew grief to the core. The death of her beloved ones made her wish death for herself with the hope of meeting them. To her, there was no sense in living. Day in and day out, she would visit the graves of her loved ones and decorate them with flowers. November was her favorite month- the month of the dead. During this time, she communed more intimately with all the people she had lost. She offered mass intentions and paid special tribute in loving memories of her deceased members. It was during these obscure moments that Nameseko came to understand the real meaning of death. It was in this perspective that, in her deepest moment of grief, she found hope. The fact that she could speak to her loved ones in a more intimate and cordial manner gave her a sense that they were not dead but were still very close to her.

All the same, most often, the absence was very strong, and she was aching because nothing could be more shocking, emotional, or final than the death of a loved one. Facing the death of someone you love, a child, a spouse, a parent, or a close friend, is one of life's most difficult experiences. You can't grasp that you've had your last visit, your last conversation, your last meal, and your last holiday with your loved one. You have regrets, desires, and unfinished business. Your mind is flooded with things you wish you had said or done. You may want to say, "I love you," one more time, and you want to hear it said to you. All these tormented her through her grieving moment. It was normal to feel this way because she had lost close to half of her dear ones, and moving on was extremely difficult.

Her warehouse of memories was filled with fond and painful remembrances as she was holding tightly to that treasured collection of fading photographs. Never for a moment did she ever feel ready to say goodbye or to deal with the grief that had overtaken her. She was not ready to move on to the stage of acceptance for her grief. In her hours of meditation, she always asked God to help her make sense out of what appeared to make no sense and to teach her the hope and light of her grief. This is what she learned during the darkest moment of her grief: Remember a few scriptural truths.

When you are dealing with grief, your emotions are high, and your thoughts are scattered. In the middle of this confusing and hard time, you need to remember a few simple truths from the Bible. God will use them to help you understand what you are experiencing and give you hooks on which to hang your emotions on. You can't prepare for the death of a loved one. Whether death results from a sudden accident or a long illness, it always catches us unprepared. Death is so deeply emotional and stunningly final that there is nothing you can do ahead of time that will help you sail through your moment of loss. Those who knew that death was coming and those who were taken completely by surprise will all go through the same process.

The Bible includes many poignant stories that mirror our experiences. The story of the death of David's son, Absalom, gives us a picture of a grieving parent.

Absalom plotted to take David's place as king of Israel. When his rebellion was crushed, he was killed, even though David had ordered his soldiers to take him alive. David knew Absalom's actions might lead to his death, but that didn't lessen his grief. 2 Samuel 18:33 tells us, "And the king was deeply moved and went up to the chamber over the gate and wept. And as he went, he said, "O my son Absalom, my son, my son Absalom! Would I have died instead of you, O Absalom, my son, my son!"

Death shakes us to the core.

David's cry is the cry of every grieving parent. Whether it is unexpected or predictable, death shakes us to the core. The pain is inescapable. Don't feel guilty or embarrassed if you feel unprepared to face it. In the story, David does not shy away from expressing his grief and inner turmoil. Though he knew his son might be killed, he was still stuck deeply by grief and loss. There's no way to be ready for what you are going through. Death was not part of God's original plan. One reason death is so hard to accept and understand is that it's completely out of step with the life God planned for this world. The apostle Paul calls death our "enemy" (1 Corinthians 15:25-26). Death is the enemy of everything good and beautiful about life. It should make you morally sad and righteously angry. Death reminds us that we live in a world that is terribly broken, not functioning according to God's original design, where life was meant to give way to life in eternity. God encourages you to mourn. Death was never meant to be. When you recognize this, you will hunger for a final restoration of all things. You will long to live in a place where the last enemy, death, has been defeated.

It's normal to feel alone.

Death is one of the loneliest experiences of human existence. The circumstances you are dealing with are individual and unique. It's normal to feel as if no one has been through what you're experiencing. It's normal to feel all alone, even when you are surrounded by people. But the death of a loved one is a universal experience, and a company of mourners surrounds you. Yet there is an even more powerful way in which you are not alone. Your Savior, Jesus, has taken another name, Emmanuel, or "God with us." This name reminds you that, as you come to Christ, you literally become the place where God dwells. You have a powerful brother, savior, counselor, and friend who not only stands beside you but lives within you. His presence makes it impossible for you to be alone in this moment of pain (John 14:15-20). Good can come out of the very worst of things. Is death a bad thing? Yes, but the Bible tells us that the brightest of good things can be found in the midst of evil's darkness.

God defeated sin and death.

The death of Jesus Christ is a powerful demonstration of this truth. On the hill of death outside the city, the best thing that ever happened came from the worst thing ever. What could be worse than the killing of the Messiah? What could be more unjust than the illegal execution of the one perfect person who ever lived? In the sermon he preached on the day of Pentecost, Peter said that Jesus' death was an evil thing done by evil men to the one truly good person in the whole world (Acts 2:22-36). But then, this terrible moment was under God's control. God planned that this ultimate evil would accomplish ultimate good. In this dark moment, as Jesus died on the cross, God defeated sin and death, two enemies we could not defeat on our own. In the same way, God can and does bring wonderful things out of the darkest moments of our lives. Your Lord is present with you in this darkness. He has planned that even the darkest of things would result in redemptive good for His children. He surrendered His Son to death so you could have life. And He will not abandon you now.

Death is an enemy, but this enemy will die.

One day, death will be put to death. The death of a loved one should remind you that God's work is not yet complete.

Because of sin, death entered the world. When sin is completely defeated, death will also be defeated. The apostle Paul talks about Christ's present ministry this way: "For he must reign until he has put all enemies under his feet. The last enemy to be destroyed is death" (1 Corinthians 15:2526). Jesus died so we would no longer have to die. When He rose from the dead, death was defeated. Until Jesus returns, we still experience death, but one day, life will not give way to death. Children will not mourn their parents. Parents will not mourn their children. There will be no widows or grieving friends. Yes, death is an enemy, but this enemy will die. The present reign of Christ guarantees this. One day, life will give way to life for eternity.

As you weep, remember that the One who weeps with you understands your heartache. He is "a man of sorrows and acquainted with grief" (Isaiah 53:3). But He does more than understand; he also acts. Jesus will not let death reign forever. On the cross, he defeated death, and his resurrection is your guarantee that one day, all who believe in him will be resurrected to a life of glory and peace. One day will come again to end physical death and to usher in a new heaven and earth where there will be no dying, no tears, and no sorrow (Revelation 21:1-4).

What you need to do.

Grieving leaves you emotionally volatile and mentally confused. It's painful in expected and unexpected ways. Death interrupts your plans and messes up your schedule. Sometimes, death brings people together and sometimes drives them apart. Death mixes the best and the worst of memories. Because death is this confusing mix of emotions and experiences, it is often hard to know exactly what to do when it has entered your door. Do not be discouraged by this, though, as there are ways in which you can tackle grieving and the concept of death. Here are some biblical directions:

Be honest about your emotions.

Being a Christian does not mean being a stoic. God doesn't want you to hide your emotions or wear a happy face mask. He wants you to come to him with complete honesty and vulnerability. In the Psalms, God invites us to bring our honest grief to him. Psalm 34:15 depicts God as a loving father, watching over his children and listening to their cries. Psalms 13, 22, 42, and 73 picture God's people running to him in grief and confusion.

Don't hide your emotions; when you are struggling, run to the one who knows you completely and loves you faithfully. As Peter says, "Cast all your anxieties on him because he cares for you." (1 Peter 5:7)

Run to where comfort can be found.

When he was suffering, the apostle Paul said an amazing thing about the Lord. "Blessed be the God and Father of our Lord Jesus Christ, the Father of mercies and God of all comfort..." (2 Corinthians 1:3). All real, lasting comfort has its source in the Lord because he is the Father of compassion and comfort. Think about this. Your heavenly Father is in charge of comfort and compassion. He exercises his loving power on earth so that comfort will be available. Whenever anyone, anytime, anywhere, experiences real comfort, it is because God, the source of all true comfort, has made it happen. It is never useless to cry out to him. He has the power to bring hope and rest to your soul in ways you could never conceive. God, in his grace, has assigned this job to himself.

Don't fall into grief's traps.

Moments of sorrow are also moments of temptation. You have an enemy who wants to use this moment to tempt you to question God's goodness and love. He will tempt you to be envious of others and to become angry and bitter. The struggle of grief is not just a struggle of sorrow but of temptation as well. Look out for grief traps. Watch yourself for signs of doubt, anger, envy, self-pity, and bitterness. When you see these things in yourself, run to Jesus for his forgiveness, strength, and protection. He will welcome you with open arms and aid you in your journey.

Open yourself up to God's helpers.

God designed life to be a community project. We need the help of others in our lives to become the people God created us to be (Eph 4:1-16 & 1 Cor 13). When your heart is breaking, and your eyes are blinded by grief, you need the help of others more than ever. The godly friends that Jesus has put in your life can help you see things you would not see by yourself. They can help you remember God's goodness when you are tempted to forget. They can exercise faith for you when your faith is weak. When you are in despair, they can bring the comfort of Christ to you. And they can gently warn you when you are tempted to get off track. Don't try to go through your sadness alone. God has placed helpers in your life. Look for them, and be patient with them. Since no human comforter is perfect, their comfort will not be perfect either.

Be thankful.

Even in the darkest of moments, you can find clear signs of God's presence and love. The apostle Paul says it this way. "Give thanks in all circumstances, for this is the will of God in

Christ Jesus for you" (1 Thes 5:18). Notice the little preposition "in" in the middle of the verse. We are called to be thankful in every situation. We have been placed in these situations for a reason and it is our task to get out of it while following the principles of God and the Bible. This doesn't mean that you will always be thankful for what you are going through, but it does mean that you can be thankful for what God is giving you to sustain you in your grief. In your darkness, there are always little lights of God's grace and love to be found. Search for those lights. Pay attention to the good things God is doing, even in this dark moment, so your grief can be mixed with heartfelt gratitude.

Don't neglect your spiritual habits.

When you are overwhelmed with sadness, it can seem pointless to pray. You may feel too weak and emotionally distracted to read the Bible, be with your Christian community, and attend public times of worship. But you need more spiritually productive habits in your life than ever. God has called you to do these things because they mature your heart and strengthen your soul. They remind you of who you are and who the Lord is. They reconnect you to your identity as his child and help you to remember that a time is coming when you won't have to face death ever again.

Celebrate eternity.

Look beyond this moment of grief to an eternity with God. When you entered God's family, you started a journey that won't end until you are with your Lord in eternity. The heartbreaking pains of life in a fallen world will someday end. The crushing sadness of death will end. Someday, your grief will be gone, and it won't return. So, as you grieve, remember what is to come and be thankful. You have a bright future that does not include sadness and death. You must keep your faith and know in your heart that you will be reunited with the ones you love.

Give away the comfort you have received.

Scripture says that God comforts us, not only to bring rest to our hearts, but equally that we can comfort others (2 Cor 1:3, 4). If you have experienced God's comfort in your time of grief, you are uniquely able to understand what a fellow griever is going through. So, what you do or say will give other mourners hope and rest. Don't hoard your comfort. Your experience has qualified you to be an active part of the army of helpers that the God of compassion sends into our broken, hurting world. Nameseko had come to the realization that remembering her loved ones, she was not alone. Jesus endured death for her so that even in the face of death, she would be able to live with hope, strength, and courage. And because of what Jesus has done for her, good things can happen even in the darkest moments of her life. She would not allow grief to rob her of life. She chose to live and experience the grace that Jesus died to give her.

CHAPTER SEVEN-

RISING ABOVE THE STORMS: FINDING HOPE IN THE MIDST OF REJECTION, ADVERSITY AND DESPAIR

In her anguish and desperation, Nameseko told herself, "Rejection is the most negative force in all of creation. It's hurtful to feel despised and rejected." The Two most powerful spiritual forces in the world are love and rejection. While love is the most positive spiritual force in the world, rejection is the most negative. Have you suffered from the hurt and pains of being rejected? So many have, and the effects can be devastating and seen everywhere. Rejection and the fear of rejection can play a major role in developing and expressing the personality and moral fiber of each of us. It can be one of the most powerful negative forces in developing one's character and well-being.

Rejection can be defined as the sense of being unwanted, unloved, and even betrayed. You desire people to love you, yet you feel or believe that they do not provide that love. Moreover, it could be that either the ones you love have or will hurt you. You want to be part of a group, but you feel excluded. Somehow, you are always on the outside looking in, trapped, unable to do what you desire most. Rejection steals the love we so deeply are in need of. Sometimes, rejection is so wounding and painful that the mind refuses to focus on it. It is in our nature to ignore or diminish it. Jesus, our Lord and Savior, knew the biting effect of rejection: Isaiah 53:3; He was despised and rejected by mankind, a man of suffering, and familiar with pain".

Like one from whom people hide their faces, he was despised, and we held him in low esteem. But rejection can be so hurtful and damaging. Nevertheless, down deep, you may know something is there, even though it may be deeper than the mind, deeper than reason, deeper than any memory. Rejection takes root in your spirit. The book of Proverbs describes this as; "A merry heart maketh a cheerful countenance: but by sorrow of the heart the spirit is broken" (Pro; 51), and Pro. 18: 14; "The spirit of a man will sustain his infirmity; but a wounded spirit who can bear?" Rejection causes a wounded spirit.

Love and rejection are emotional and spiritual.

The most powerful positive spiritual force in the universe is the love of God. As the scriptures say in 1 John 4:8, 16: "The one who does not love does not know God, for God is love. And we have come to know and have believed God has love for us. God is love, and the one who abides in love abides in God. God abides in him, and he is in God." God is love; therefore, love is God's most powerful force. If love is the most powerful positive spiritual force in creation, it follows that lack of love is the most powerful negative spiritual force in creation. Rejection is the denial or betrayal of love and acceptance in our lives. It is one of the most painful, the most neglected, yet the most common emotional wounds from which we suffer.

When someone has suffered from the trauma of rejection and has a spirit of rejection, two things happen: (1). They reject themselves, which is referred to as "Self-rejection." (2). They live with and are guided by the Spirit of the "Fear of rejection." Both are very powerful and controlling forces in one's life. Proverbs 15:13 says, "A joyful heart makes a cheerful face, but when the heart is sad, the spirit is broken. One of the products of rejection is a broken spirit. Proverbs 17:22 says, "A joyful heart is a good medicine, but a broken spirit dries up the bones." A broken spirit, brought about by rejection, is capable of "drying up," or taking away the desire for life" Proverbs 18:14, adds; "The spirit of a man can endure his sickness, but a broken spirit who can bear?"

If the desire for life has gone, there is no chance for healing to take place. The Spirit of rejection can become the dominant, controlling spirit in one's life. When someone is rejected and thus self-rejected, they often develop low selfesteem, a poor self-concept, a fantasy friend or friend, multiple personalities, paranoia, and suspicion of other people and institutions. They then can live in a fantasy world that they can slip into during times of stress. In this fantasy world, they can often find peace because they are accepted and not rejected. They can be "in control" because the fear of rejection does not threaten them. A child never picks up a rejection spirit, receiving unconditional love, care, and understanding. Something bad is always going on in a child's life when the spirit of rejection is brought in. A glaring example is when two parents get divorced, and the rejection spirit comes in constantly telling the child that they are not loved and that it was their fault.

There is medical scientific evidence that a fetus in the womb senses rejection. There is also a large body of experiential evidence that a fetus can be affected painfully by rejection way before birth. The Spirit of rejection can enter a person at or shortly after conception. Yes, parents or a single parent can and sometimes do reject their children in the womb. Prenatal emotional traumas can cause rejection when emotionally or verbally expressed during a pregnancy.

It isn't for nothing that God has given us perfect instructions for a healthy and whole family to operate. The head of the household must honor Christ and his teachings above all others. Then he honors his wife above himself and then his children and himself, in that order. When the husband takes time and has his priorities right, He and his wife's relationship with the children is loving, balanced, and healthy. It takes time and a caring heart to listen, even though you may not totally understand the other person's emotions. Any other order opens up the door for the enemy, and the results can be anger, fear, guilt, shame, and resentment.

Nameseko reacted to the wounds of rejection she received early for her entire life. The Fear of rejection haunted her. Rejection wounded her spirit. This is because she was wounded at an early age, and she was reacting to those wounds. Without being delivered from this bondage, her spirit never healed and was always suffering. The trap was always set for a revolving door to a counselor or doctor for the magic medicine to cure her pain.

Sometimes, rejection is so wounding and painful that the mind refuses to focus on it. Nevertheless, Nameseko knew something was there even though it was deeper than the mind, deeper than the reason, deeper than the memory. It was in her spirit. The book of Proverbs describes this as: "A merry heart maketh a cheerful countenance: but by sorrow of the heart the spirit is broken" (Pro. 5: 13); "The spirit of a man will sustain his infirmity; but a wounded spirit who can bear?" (Pro. 18: 14). A vibrant, free spirit helps a person through great difficulties, but a crushed or wounded spirit has a crippling effect in all areas of life.

All fear is spiritual in nature. There is a second spirit that takes hold from rejection, called the "Fear of rejection" spirit. This spirit hindered Nameseko from having full and healthy relationships with God and all those she loved. Once present, the Spirit of rejection causes emotional and mental havoc.

Nameseko experienced rejection all her life. These are the symptoms of a demonic spirit of rejection at work that was hovering around her life. She suffered from a couple of many. She always brought all these to the Lord and asked for revelation on their cause to see if their source was rejection.

She realized she was dealing with the spirit of rejection and that God could free her and heal her.

She was always having to prove herself worthy. She felt loneliness, self-pity, self-doubting, defeatism, misery, addiction, depression and anxiety, despair or hopelessness, paranoia, schizophrenia, death, or suicide. All of which were also called psychological afflictions or issues. As her ordeal got worse, Big Pharma and psychotherapists made billions of dollars in treating her. The primary consequence of the spirit of rejection is the inability to receive healthy love from others and to communicate true love to them in a wholesome, healthy way.

Nameseko had never been told and shown that she was loved. That is why, for her, rejection was one of the greatest hindrances to divine love. However, she allowed God to work in her life to bring her to the knowledge of his divine love and how to love the ones she loved and cherished in a Godly and Holy way. And hope maketh not ashamed; because the love of God is shed abroad in our hearts by the Holy Ghost which is given unto us. (Romans 5:5). Love is never disappointed when fixed and centered in God. In God's love, He withholds nothing. God's love is perfect.

Simply recognizing and accepting what Christ had done for her brought so much relief and released her from the spirit of rejection. The act of forgiveness is absolutely necessary in getting healed from a traumatic rejection. Nameseko took more direct deliverance action to rid herself of the controlling spirit of rejection. The Lord, her sustainer, did declare to her to 'be healed of the effects of being rejected,' and she was healed. She stands to testify to the powerful work of God in life, and as a healed soul, she shares her healing journey with us. May the Holy Spirit help you identify how or where rejection has wounded you. Try writing it down; it is important that you try to identify the person, people, or institution that caused your rejection.

Forgive all those involved in rejecting you. Truly forgive them. This can be very hard but absolutely necessary in getting healed. Forgiveness is a very powerful healing tool.

There is the possibility of deliverance from the bondage and grasp of the demonic. Bring it to him and allow him to do what he does best. He is here with you to help you. Share with God honestly, and let him heal you. Tell God what happened to you and how you feel. Focus on him and his faithfulness. Spend time with him, and let him restore where sin and rejection have been destroyed. Forgiveness releases God's divine healing power and removes the ground that allows the spirit of rejection to keep a hold of you. Then she prayed, 'Father, I wait now for you to bring to my mind, through the Holy Spirit's ministry, any specific person or situation I need to forgive. I would like to forgive. Specifically, forgive each person or situation that rejected you. Father, your Word says that whoever calls on your name shall be delivered. I ask now for deliverance from the curses and effects of bitterness in my life, and I do now renounce and rebuke the unclean spirits involved. I Cast Out all spirits of Unforgiveness, Anger, Violence, Hatred, Rejection, Fear, Retaliation, Murder, And Memory Recall of All Offenses Against Me. I curse the roots, the Spirits of Rejection and unforgiveness, in the name of Jesus Christ, to wither and dry up to its roots and never again bear fruit in my life.

In the name of Jesus and by the power of His Blood, I break every curse that has come upon me and my family because of Rejection, unforgiveness, and all of their effects. Under the authority of His Blood, I renounce, rebuke, and cast out all unclean spirits of rejection, guilt, condemnation, unworthiness, shame, infirmities, and fears that have come in because of a bitter heart. I stand now, believing I am forgiven, knowing there is no condemnation in Christ Jesus. I am forgiven and have been washed clean by the power of the Blood of Jesus. Father. I am loved. I am your child. Thank you, Jesus, for cleansing us from all the effects of rejection, unforgiveness, and bitterness. Amen!

One thing about Nameseko was that her trials had made her closer to God. Her spirit was arrested, and she had this intimacy with God that she found Him her closest and best companion. She spent quality time alone with God. She talked to God every second of her life, and when she could not find the answers, that baffled her life. As she often prayed for God's forgiveness to those that rejected her she found eternal peace in Christ. She continued in prayers of deliverance from the hooks of rejection and unforgiveness; "Father in heaven, I behold you as God of all the heavens and earth. I believe you sent your only begotten Son to destroy the works of the flesh and the devil. I believe Jesus, the son of man, died on a cruel cross like a common criminal. I believe that he shed his precious blood to absolve me of my personal sins, the sins of my parents of my forefathers, and the sins of the world, to wash us clean and heal us. I thank you, Father, in heaven, for raising Jesus from the dead to live forever as my savior, my Lord, and my God.

Thank you, Father, for sending the Holy Spirit to set all of those apart who receive Him as the baptizer, the Comforter, and the One who empowers us to live the life of a true believer. Father, in the Name of Jesus Christ and under the power of His Blood, I confess that I and those of my family as far back as Adam have not loved but have rejected and resented certain people or groups who have hurt, slandered, offended, betrayed, or disappointed us.

I have held unforgiveness, bitterness, prejudices, hatred, anger, rage, desire for retaliation, emotional memories, and murder in my heart. I confess I have caused hurt to others by my behavior and lack of love. You have told me in your Word that to be forgiven, I must forgive. I choose to obey your Word; I choose to forgive individually and on behalf of all those in my family tree, all those carrying the spirit of rejection. I choose to forgive all those who rejected me. Please give me the grace and power to forgive Father.

Father, I plead the blood of Jesus on all those in my family lineage for the power of your healing love to be poured out upon them. As God of the living, who lives outside of time, I pray you would bring all of my parent's generations before you that we may be absolved of our curses of unforgiveness and rejection. I rebuke and break all curses brought upon myself and my family because of any and all spirits of rejection.

I forgive (my mother, father, or figure of authority that rejected me). It is only because you first loved me that I can forgive. Thank you, Jesus! I declare and confirm my and our forgiveness to Each and every person, living or dead, who has rejected me in any way, hurt, disappointed, betrayed, failed, abused, or caused unjust pain to me.

Nameseko learned during deep spiritual encounters to release her offenders to God as she prayed. Repent of your desire to punish or take revenge. Let God deal with the offense. Focus on today rather than the past. Let the offender off the hook. Declare God as judge over the person and the situation. "Do not take revenge, my friends, but leave room for God's wrath, for it is written: 'It is mine to avenge; I will repay,' says the lord" (Romans 12:19). "Bless those who persecute you; bless and do not curse" (Romans 12:14).

God will give us the grace to fully set everyone free. May we be like Jesus, who was the first to love. When God forgives us, He gives us the power to forgive. May the river of God's life flow through us so that we may bless everyone. "Forgiveness is the very spirit of heaven removing the hiding places of demonic activity from the caverns of the human soul. It is every wrong made right, and every evil made void. The power released in forgiveness is actually a mighty weapon in the war to save our soul."

When we ask the Lord, in Jesus Christ's name, He assures us with His peace and understanding. If for any reason you question your salvation, go to a quiet place, alone, and talk to Jesus. Repent of your sins and commit your life to Him. He is faithful. He always listens and always responds. Nameseko never stopped trusting God and believing in His plan.

She knew the storm was intense. She knew the waves seemed a mile high. She knew that destruction seemed imminent, but she also knew this: there was a shoreline that graced the ocean's end. Every wave will eventually reach the sandy solitude, whether in crashing waves or flat seas. It all returns to the same place: the shoreline of His will. Don't be afraid of the storm. She didn't have to keep treading on water. She just needed to float and trust the tides of His hands.

There isn't a single woman in the bible that God used who "had it easy." Ruth didn't have it easy, Esther didn't have it easy, Sarah didn't have it easy, Hannah didn't have it easy, and Bathsheba didn't have it easy. Mary didn't have it easy. The woman at the well and the woman with the issue of blood certainty didn't have it easy. God's daughters don't have it easy, but they have the anointing. They have it appointed. They have been highly favored. They have been predestined. And every woman God used has had the victory. Walk in your anointing and watch God work!

Nameseko was not crazy. It had all been real, and it stretched her and, at times, seemed as if she had been crushed down to death.

Their words broke her heart.

Their actions broke her trust.

That disease broke her body.

That illness broke her hope.

That circumstance broke her spirit.

But God...

He came to overcome it all.

And guess what?

It never broke her!

It challenged her, and it lost!

She is still here. She is not "just" a survivor. She is a fighter. She is a warrior. And yes, she may be covered in scars and tears, but they are scars of death's defeat! Her scars have become a memoir of her soul's journey, telling only a story of triumph!

You see, they did not see her the same way anymore because a warrior was birthed from the destruction and fires in her life. What was meant to kill her didn't. And while they kept judging her for starting over, others clapped because she never quit. She entered the flames covered in life's grit but came out of the fire polished in God's grace. The abuse, pain, anxiety, bullying, fear, anguish, doubt, worry, crushing, pulling words, moments, days, and years were real, but so were her strength and resilience. She survived everything they said she wouldn't. She is still standing, and she is remarkable. Glory be to God!

She is not the ashes and rubble suffocating beneath a fading fire. No! She is the gold being refined by the blaze of the flames. She may not look like much going in, but she won't look or be the same coming out. He is raising up a new remnant. Yes, her calling was going to crush her! She knew that if she was called to mend the brokenhearted, she was going to wrestle with a broken heart.

True, if you are called to heal God's little ones, you are going to experience your own share of trauma.

If you're called to preach and teach the gospel, you will be sifted for the wisdom that anoints your message. If you are called to empower, your self-esteem will be attacked- your successes hard fought.

Your calling will come with spiritual warfare and a sifting. Both are necessary for your mantle to be authentic, humble and powerful.

Your crushing won't be easy because your assignment is not easy, and you can't minister powerfully what you haven't walked out. Read that sentence again.

When you're feeling the weight of it coming down on you, run to the Father who longs to be your comfort. Let him whisper your true identity over you while resting under the shadow of his wings. Position yourself against his heartbeat. Let him renew your strength and set your eyes forward. Always keep in mind that: No olives, no oil, no grapes, no wine. Your oil is not cheap, my friend.

Yes, Nameseko's life's battles seemed to be relentless, and the feeling of loss was crippling and paralyzing, but whenever she walked with Christ, she was never broken. He was her portion, and she was more than a conqueror. Yes, she was wounded all her life, but she was never beyond repair, for the great "I Am" knows her by name, and with Him, she could not and will not fail. She continued to walk out of the lion dens unharmed. She continued to defeat the Goliaths in her life. She continued to be blessed even in and through the mess. She belonged to him, and at all times, she received his promises.

CHAPTER EIGHT-

THE SEED OF TRUE GREATNESS: LIVING YOUR TRUE PURPOSE

Although Nameseko had faced many challenges in her life, she always tackled them with grace. Being a mother enhanced her compassionate and virtuous nature. You could depend on her to support you through it all. Nameseko always focused on dedication and hard work as a tool for success, and her story can really be a source of motivation as you go after your goals with that same determination. This is because there is nothing in life more powerful than a woman with a purpose (Coach Mélissa, 2018).

The greatest failure you can suffer is not to have tried. Nameseko was everything that grace and greatness could speak of. There was something within her that yearned for greatness. All she ever wanted was the meaning of her life to be more than just a few sentences engraved on a tombstone. She believed that God wrote the script of her story that required her to do great things and then planted those seeds within her. God's plan was to make her truly great for her entire generation. How this would look in this age and in the future was something she tried to figure out with God and herself.

Nameseko was a woman of God who waited patiently as her roots grew deep into God's word and promises. As the seasons continued to change, she grew unshakable in her faith, and when the winds and storms of life came as they always did, they were never able to destroy her.

Sure, a few branches were tattered, broken, or pruned away, but her deep roots beneath the visible losses held her upright, even though she swayed with the winds of troubled times. And when the old leaves spiraled away, they never left her empty and lifeless. Instead, they offered her a chance for new growth. The color will return and the growing pains will ease, for she trusts her Creator, as he had never failed her.

Although Nameseko was often colorless in this dreadfully gray and fallen world, her spirit was as vibrant as the eternity she knew awaited her. She went into so many battles time and time again and somehow came out of the storms of life brighter than before, being refined by the fire and polished by the grit. Her challenges strengthened her, and her opposition came hard at her, but God upheld her time and again. Nameseko would die for anyone she loved. So often, she even loved others long before she ever learned to love herself. It took her all too long to realize that she was capable of loving others and herself simultaneously. She lived and suffered boldly so that others would know that even though the pain was real, healing too was, and that hope is never fully lost but only temporarily forgotten. She was a warrior. Her body and mind tested her relentlessly, but she never submitted to its stubborn declarations of brokenness and defeat, for her God had already clothed her in victory. Her flesh was just a vessel to something that truly couldn't be contained, housed, or caged. After all, she used the cracks life inflicted, as light sources to empower others. She shined from the inside out, and all who got to see her struggles also saw her overcome. She didn't just see the battle. She trusted in what was beyond the battle. She wanted to be a witness and testament to true beauty and true strength for it was God within her that shined- not her, and with Him, she would never and could never fail. She- is YOU!

Nameseko was multitalented and had a sound education in social sciences, international relations, human psychology, human resources, and humanitarianism. All this helped her to know how to navigate life's challenges and turmoil. From all her studies on human ingenuity, you could call her a trusted friend in a complicated world. Some of her worldclass stories can be derived from her childhood experiences and academic and professional background. Some years ago, while researching how technology can help the world's most failed state, Nameseko found herself amidst the darkness of human tragedy. "I realized that the internet is going to be at the epicenter of terrorism, persecution, and organized crime," she said. Once back safe and sound in her own country, she was inspired to create an online platform that applies digital advertising technology to reach and discourage people from joining armed groups, a challenge that requires persistence and empathy. "When the internet is used to harm, it is women who are the most affected. Women are more likely than their male counterparts to be attacked online for their opinions."

Inspired by her experiences as a woman growing up in a typical patriarchal society where women faced marginalization and oppression, she started a non-profit organization as founder and CEO of Women DREAM. Nameseko helped women and girls in her community and around the world to access quality education.

A recipient of several communities, leadership, peace, and Humanitarian Awards, she believes that when a girl is educated, there are fewer occurrences of abuse and violence going down, making the world a healthier and safer place for all. "A child born to a mother who can read is 50 percent more likely to survive beyond the age of 5," she said. Currently, the organization's focus is on empowering women and girls in poor rural communities, where research and her work showed that girls were most at risk.

During her recent work in poor rural communities, Women DREAM created a media and leadership platform in war-affected zones and refugee camps, and their recent Center of Worth helps adolescent girls stay in school and provides social, emotional, and academic counseling, health education, and financial and digital literacy training.

Nameseko was a victim and survivor in every sense of the word. Her life's experiences inspired her to make survivors feel heard.

Raising the voices of young women both here and overseas who have survived violence and overcome other struggles became her mission in life. "I was doing fieldwork in TUKWA Territory when young people began seeking me out and asking me to help them share their experiences with youth in other communities," said Nameseko. "I knew what I was doing went beyond research, that there was potential for combining empathy, compassion, and connection with a new approach to human suffering." She focused on the power of narrative, compassion, and connection in individual and community development. "Knowing your own suffering can help others feel less lonely is also a basic humanitarian need." Give yourself a boost of self-confidence by memorizing your own pains and suffering. It serves a great deal.

Nameseko's creativity, resilience, and remarkable stories prevalently created stories that exemplify the ultimate power of womanhood while adding charm to her unique existence. Passionately making ends meet and fiercely creating history in her own world, she worked relentlessly to structure her ideas. She was an inspirational woman who had redefined her enthusiasm for women's empowerment. She was renowned for her research and findings in formulating and redefining the world of abused women and girls and had set a groundbreaking foundation with International recognition.

Her equation with success prominently made her one of the thriving experts in the industry of creating change and transformation in a typically dark and chaotic world.

After graduating in social science and humanities, she completed her fieldwork on social justice for vulnerable and displaced women and girls. She joined her friends and successfully captivated the attention of many through her unmatchable expertise and affection for the marginalized. Coming with a refined mindset, she built a huge network of trusted, compassionate and a specialized social media agency in the world of human fraternity. The rarest and luxury collection of beautiful souls in her network has become the trusted brands that have been growing ceaselessly and with a deep dedication and passion to serve humanity.

Nameseko was voted the most outstanding, iconic, influential woman and peace crusader of 2020 by the Sunlight Digital Journal. She was equally awarded a highly prestigious international award for speaking up for the voiceless and oppressed. Nameseko helped adult children who had been negatively impacted by their childhood experiences learn to discover the subconscious patterns and reactive behaviors that kept them stuck. She was also one of the most listened-to speakers on Insight Timer and a top Life Coach.

She developed online courses for those who wished to learn to set boundaries, heal their inner child, and recover from toxic codependent relationships. She also had a top-ranking podcast called Breakdowns to Breakthroughs. Her 12-week Breakthrough Coaching Program has helped thousands of adult children heal from Adult Children of Alcoholics (ACOA) issues and childhood emotional neglect. Her tagline is, "It's Not You—It's Your Programming." All these she owed to her childhood experiences and upbringing.

Nameseko was a philanthropist, an author, a model, and a sought-after motivational speaker who had managed to inspire countless women from her candid life experiences. She was a lifelong model who powerfully recovered from aggressive masculinity. She knotted her harrowing experiences of going from dependence on outer beauty to embracing her woes, tragedies, illnesses, and scars toward her new life of influencing women all over the world. Led by her life experiences and optimism, she had been passing on hope and support for women going through abusive relationships and other trials.

Nameseko was on the board of two non-profits, RISEWOMEN and GIRLS EXCHANGE PROGRAM, which offers livelihoods to women living in poverty and denial of resources, and People of Purpose, whose mission is to change the world. With her powerful drive to work, Nameseko successfully continued her journey as a model while strongly adding value to society.

As a modern mother and philanthropist, her courageous experiences highlight the work of those opening the heart space to inspire others and build a better environment. Since its creation, her initiative has grown to include a worldwide network of thousands of different individuals who all believe in transforming human lives through her unique virtual and onsite education platform.

Nameseko had traveled widely and had reinvented the business world with her sparkling approaches to adding value as a business coach. Her expertise and experience were an added charm to her methods and made her a sought-after speaker. Known for her vibrant personality, she led hundreds of leaders and entrepreneurs who felt shame, overwhelmed, fear and intimidation by the public to be a beacon of transformation for those they serve. Leveraging social media's ultimate power, she extensively influenced and led businesses toward their successful endeavors. In fact, her commitment to her community placed her in various leadership roles that inspired growth in multiple lives.

Also, Nameseko was best known as a global speaker, influencer co-host of Good Morning, Deep Divers, and a certified human rights and social justice expert. While bringing her honest stories to the table, Nameseko had enthusiastically uncovered the candid details about being a thriving soul in life's hardest battles. Driven by her life motto, 'Be brave, be you,' her blog, beingnameseko.org, highlights her personality and the moments that define her. With a goal to strongly stand against the conventional norms and "taboos" within her patriarchal communities, her prominence has caught the attention of numerous people.

Nameseko was an expert with 20+ years of experience, a fourth-time award-winning women's leadership advocate who transformed women's careers through her public speaking, training, and coaching at the local, national, and international levels - all while raising and mentoring her three daughters. As a seasoned coach and educator, she created POWERVOICE - an online school that teaches coaches and consultants how to ethically market themselves and their businesses. She was a trained brain-behavior marketing specialist, personal brand strategist, fervent believer in the power of mentorship and storytelling. She just launched another blog series entitled "Catalyst" - microstories featuring the trials and triumphs of coaches who believe in the life-changing impact of role models.

While her prominence and creativity had been impressing the world, her presence had substantially inspired numerous young hustlers. If someone is looking for motivation and positivity, they can certainly draw immense inspiration from her unconventional journey.

CHAPTER NINE-

SUCCESS COMES
WITH GREAT PAINS

Nameseko was an achiever and an acclaimed visionary leader. She had earned great respect and reputation. Despite what she had been through and what society had gotten her through, she rose to be a founder of an International Charity, a non-profit organization and the Executive Managing Director. Despite the hurdles and challenges in her life, she proved to be an outstanding leader. Her desires and wishes were ever to touch lives and serve humanity given her sufferings in life. She wanted to give back to her community and society the best of herself and to be a source of encouragement and inspiration to others who faced immeasurable storms in life. She had risen to be a wellrespected and renowned woman.

Many called her the mother of humanity, a role model, a voice for the voiceless, defender for the defenseless, fearless and courageous leader. She was well accomplished, with a polished education from a noble, humble, and poor background. This only kept her humble and true to herself.

She never stopped thanking God for raising her from the ashes and rubble of life to a beacon of hope to many, from chaos to clarity. It was not by might nor by her power but by the special grace and spirit of the Lord. Her greatest desire was to be a blessing to others. She was passionate about making a difference in the world **by helping communities and individuals prepare for and recover from humanmade and natural disasters. For this,** she was willing to pay any prize, for this was not just a profession but a Calling and a Ministry.

What exactly had this incredible woman been through? Her story was unique. Many think that getting to the top is a license to be exonerated from hardships, trials, and tragedies. Having a good education, getting married, having kids, getting the best jobs, living in well-furnished homes, and driving the best cars—all these and many other life achievements—are never an exoneration of life's pains and dark moments. For every great mission, the preparation is a great trial.

One day, Nameseko sat in her office, and her mind took her back to memory lane. The hardships she had endured, the fires that burnt her, the rivers she crossed, and the top mountains she climbed all stared at her as she recollected every pain and bitter water she had drunk from. She had faced child abuse and neglect, denial of opportunities, and harmful cultural and patriarchal tendencies that made her regret why she was born a woman.

Even as a leader and mentor, her troubles did not end. Rather they were increasing in geometric proportion. After all her achievements in life, she was still battling with more excruciating challenges. Her myriad torments included raising successful children in the fear and ways of the Lord. She was deeply worried about the future of her kids and loved ones. Her children were all grown up and were soon going to live independently from her. She wanted the best for them and never allowed anyone of them to experience what she went through. She made sure she multitasked just to give them the best. She always reminded herself that if anything should happen to her children in this life, she would kill herself. This alone puts her in constant fear, panic, and anxiety.

Another pain that took Nameseko was her constant flashbacks and cruel emotional abuse of her feeling unworthy as a woman. Sean constantly reminded her that she was good for nothing. Everything she was and had achieved meant nothing as long as she was his wife. She would often hear words like shame! I made you who you are! Ungrateful bitch! She lived most of her life on the defensive, trying to defend herself or prove her worth just because of the abusive words that she had heard all of her life. All these made her live in a perpetual fear, lack of self-confidence, always afraid to make mistakes. Her defense was always to seek perfection and public validation. These were clear signals of low selfesteem. To make things worse, she faced wicked opposition and cruel criticism from detractors. Her inability to respond to all the sufferings and needs of her loved ones, her failing health, and her fear of failing compounded to make her an emotional wreck.

According to Nameseko, going through narcissistic abuse was really a lonely experience. It is not like other relationships. There are so many different dynamics. You deal with lies, manipulation, infidelity, verbal and psychological or other kinds of abuse, trauma, loss of selfesteem, and deception. And even as she meditated on this, she knew the only people who would really understand what she was talking about were the people that have gone through it.

This is not just a bad relationship experience; it is the dismantling and destruction of one's life, one piece at a time. As you are trying desperately to put it together, people who don't understand rather than helping, look at you as if you are going crazy. And in weird ways, it feels like you are. When a relationship is slowly breaking you apart, it's a difficult and horrible experience to go through. She would wish this does not happen to anyone.

Pain is the most common illness experienced on the planet, yet those who suffer are often treated poorly and may be stigmatized for feeling pain. When you stub your toe, you yell, ow, and feel pain! However, when pain is emotional, mental, and spiritual, society tends to view it differently. Known as the dark night of the soul, the storm, the suffering serves a purpose. It endows you with vital resources for personal growth. The happiest people are those who have undergone hardship to emerge with deep wisdom to share with others. Your attitude and mental resilience measure your response to hardship and how you interpret how events shape your life. When facing hardships, there are only two choices: rise to the challenge and overcome them, or retreat into despair.

What is the point of pain? The Centre states that we are foolish to think that modern science can banish pain altogether. It is designed to be protective, an alarm system.

Suffering affects both personal and professional lives and when not dealt with, pain negatively affects our well-being. If you are not going through some form of suffering now, chances are someone closer to you is. Some therapists speak about the myths, truths, and growth in suffering by posing the question: 'How do you suffer well?' In other words, how do you grow through suffering? Suffering initiates a search for significance. It is important to make sense of it and find meaning and purpose in suffering. We all need one another, and nothing is certain or uncertain; they are both illusions. Humans cannot predict exactly what is going to occur, so letting go of the sureness of an outcome brings vulnerability. Sharing experiences and emotions is healthy. When you suffer, you need to talk about your experience, and part of becoming a loving person leads to receiving love.

When suffering appears, and one chooses to grow through suffering, sensitivity and empathy occur. You are no longer lost in your own pain but rather quick to help others get through their own suffering. You have to process your own pain enough to be able to focus on others to respond with compassion.

Nameseko had experienced a tremendous doss of adverse childhood experiences that linked up to her adulthood. She came to understand that the purpose of all these were to lead her to self-efficacy and resilience. Once she got her score, she paid attention to her suffering and pondered, "I have endured a lot of suffering, and in that pain, here I am, existing, happy, successful, doing, creating, sharing, loving, and grateful. Without these hard times, I wouldn't have been the person I am right now, beautiful and empowered". This she told herself. Instead of thinking of yourself as a victim, think of yourself as a victor. You may never know how powerful your words and actions are or ever realize the impact they make on other's lives. Empowerment is an unstoppable force for good.

A few words from a loved one or a stranger can change the way you think and proceed. Nameseko told herself: "Bliss is found when one let go of satisfying personal and material needs, and instead, allows life to simply flow." In the words of Helen Keller, "*character cannot be developed in ease and quiet. Only through experience of trial and suffering can the soul be strengthened, ambition inspired, and success achieved*".

From her experience, Nameseko affirmed that those who have suffered have a greater capacity for understanding themselves and their surroundings. This understanding is what leads to greatness. On the mountains of truth you can never climb in vain: either you will reach a point higher up today, or you will be training your powers so that you will be able to climb higher tomorrow. Suffering is a necessary ingredient for greatness. Those who are able to weather the trials and tribulations of life are the ones who will be able to achieve the most success. She was a living testimony of "why and how suffering leads to greatness"- The role of suffering in creating a masterpiece.

According to Nameseko, art is created out of suffering. She attests that great art represents a person's most deeply held and personal thoughts and feelings and that through pain we can develop our true potential. While some may find this argument dark, Nameseko believed that great art is nothing, if not beautiful, in its complexity and darkness. "I overcame myself, the sufferer; I carried my own ashes to the mountains; I invented a brighter flame for myself" Nameseko believed that it is only through facing and overcoming challenges that artists can truly create something great. While some may find her philosophy depressing, her experience shows that greatness comes from within and cannot be bought or achieved easily.

For her, suffering is ultimately a positive experience, as it leads to increased understanding and creativity. In the end, art is about expressing ourselves authentically, and nothing can be done better than going through hardship. Her life was a complex reflection of enduring human suffering and, at times, very controversial. She said, "Suffering is the father of all things." According to her, the importance of enduring and overcoming suffering lies at the heart of her masterpiece.

It is through overcoming suffering that we create our own unique role in the world. This process of creation is essential for finding meaning in life; in Her deepest thoughts, "She who has endured pain her whole life, at last she found relief from it and looked down upon it with astonishment, saying: 'What was that? Was that also life?'" She believed that individuals who are able to overcome the difficulties and tribulations of life, experience a unique form of greatness.

By facing struggles head-on, artists, doctors, teachers, philosophers, and others can create works that have a lasting impact on society. Through experiencing pain and adversity, they learn to find strength in themselves. This ultimately makes them better people and stronger creators.

Nameseko's modus operandi was to turn suffering into a source of strength. She believed that suffering is a natural part of life and that it can be turned into a source of strength. She was a great motivational storyteller and often made this reference:

"That which does not kill us makes us stronger." But according to her, this was an opportunity to turn our suffering into a source of strength. She argues that if we learn to resist our pain and accept it as part of life, we can become stronger people. In fact, she often said that the only way to overcome our sufferings is by facing them head-on and learning from them.

One must learn to identify with their own pain and not rely on others for validation. When we are able to see ourselves in our pain and suffering, we can better understand our own motivations and strengths; Nameseko's life depicted every word: "She who does not know her own heart will never find her way." She recommends using pain and anguish as stepping stones to achieving greatness. The ability to turn suffering into a source of strength is one of the most important skills a person can possess. If we run away from our problems, we will only make them worse. Instead, we should learn to embrace our suffering and use it as a means of growth. This is why people who are able to turn their suffering into something positive are the strongest ones around.

Nameseko learned how to find strength in herself, which became invaluable in the face of difficulties later on in her life. We are all made of the same clay, and when we are faced with difficulty, we can learn and grow. Struggles force us to confront our weaknesses and strengths. They also teach us about ourselves and help us become wiser. In the end, suffering leads to greatness because it makes us better people. In spite of these many giants on her path, her greatest strength that made her outstanding and successful in her life was believing in herself and her ambitions. Success comes with great pains and sacrifice believing in yourself and the power to achieve your goal is a key factor to success. Life is an irony, but we only hold on to the great dreams and visions that we do soliloquy all day upon. Aspire to tell your testimony and be a hero.

CHAPTER TEN-

EPILOGUE

BE A FINISHER AMIDST THE STORMS

Each of us is given a race to run and we're called to finish our race strong. May we hold fast to the end and have faith to finish well.

Namesake is an ordinary young woman who tells her story through the darkness and the ugliest moments of pain and anguish in her life. Rather than choosing to be limited, pushed down by the storms in her life, she sees life beyond the dark clouds and chaos. She braved every obstacle and forged to the top as an Executive Managing Director and leading woman. She named her scars and turned them into stars.

As a child she has known the bitter pains of child neglect and abuse. As an adolescent and a young adult, she lived through rejection, isolation and loneliness. As a woman, she faced harsh realities of marital strife, subjugation, suppression, domestic violence, patriarchal oppression, societal conceptions, shame, humiliation, cruel opposition, and guilt defined the later part of her life. From the shame of adversity, she thrived to become a beacon of HOPE for the universe. Her light today radiates from the dark rubbles of every human struggle, pain, and brokenness. Her life is tested as she goes into battle time and again, and somehow comes brighter than before, being refined by the fire and polished by the grit. Her challenges strengthen her, and her opposition comes hard at her, but her faith upholds her time and again.

Nameseko lived and suffered boldly so that others would know that even though the pain was real, healing too was, and hope is never fully lost, only temporarily forgotten. Like a warrior never giving up when faced with life's tragedies, her body and mind tested her relentlessly, but she never submitted to its stubborn declarations of brokenness and defeat for her God had already clothed her in victory. Her flesh was just a vessel to something that truly couldn't be contained, caged or housed. Instead, she used the cracks life inflicted as light sources to empower others. She shined from the inside out, and all who got to see her struggle also saw her overcome. She didn't just see the battle. She trusted in what was beyond the battle. She wanted everyone who had ever seen her spirit to see life the same way again. She wanted to be a witness and testament to true beauty and true strength, for it was God within her that shined- not her, and with him, she will never and could never fail.

Nameseko's ministry was boldly established and the Lord was writing her testimony! She was often in a serious dilemma and in a state of contemplation- Pursuing her ordained ministry or bowing to the limitations set by her immediate environment, the opposition, and the people therein? Each time she had a mission or task, she had to face the devil and the deep blue sea. She would only have to fight through tears and heaviness to carry out the mission.

Nameseko would often be reminded that she was a married woman, a wife and a mother. Her place was in the home to take care of her children and husband. This chapter of Nameseko's life was like injuring her old wounds, how she had been treated to look like a slave in the eyes of her children, family members, friends, and sometimes outsiders.

This often left her shaking, incoherent and terrified. Faced with strong patriarchal tendencies, powerful, influential personality, her voice was often silenced through intimidation, manipulation and insults. She was always at a crossroads, confused, soaked in the pressure of constant humiliation. Each time, an announcement of success for her came with fiercer opposition and confrontation.

She never knew how to be happy whenever she received any good news because it was definitely going to come with too much tension and emotional distress. Behind every one of her success stories was a deep scar of deep pain she had endured. She often told herself, "I am not good at handling these emotional pressures." Her mental state was deteriorating under the too many mental and psychological pressures she had experienced.

In spite of all these, giving in to negativity and adversity was far from her. She knew that adversity and problems were all factors of life, and no one escaped troubles, not even the most powerful. To lose hope and faith in humanity was never a goal for Nameseko. She had to confront the trials which were truly hard. The struggles? Oh, they were very real. The pain and wounds? Whew! Run deep. But guess what? All things work together for good for Nameseko for she believed she was the true daughter of a king. The crushing was real and hard. The labor was not easy. The birthing wasn't comfortable, but what God had established came forth, and it stood as a symbol and testament to his glory, power, and love- forever and ever!

Nameseko never bargained for her woes and calamities, nor was she looking to be fixed, saved, or completed. Her God had made her a finished product by refining her through the fires of shame and humiliation. Not because she tried to be mysterious or complex but because her soul had longed to be immersed in God's deep connections and passionate love. She's tried the ordinary lackluster love, and it always left her unfulfilled. Her road was a hard journey, though she'd never ask for anyone's pity.

She had come to a place of self-love, self-confidence, and self-compassion. The seasons of hardship bore down on her soul and trembled her foundation and her faith; she held on to His promises, reminding herself that she does not have to see in order to be led. It is there, often in the darkest of days, that His voice speaks loudest. The chaos from the world around her was drowned out by a black veil, and she was left only to envision His face and listen for His voice.

Just as the disciples stood in their boat as a storm moved them all ways and the winds whirled around them, Jesus appeared before them still- and as they fixed their eyes upon Him, the magnitude of the storm no longer mattered. It was the recognition that life was not within their control, and not only accepting that but welcoming it, that kept their boat and lives from overturning.

Just as some seasons are more comfortable for us than others, life's largest transformations rarely occur in the comforts of our salvation—they lie on the outskirts and dwell in the core of challenges, propelling us to go ahead in faith instead of relying on our own ideas and false sense of logic.

To Nameseko, God has always appeared in her eleventh hour, on the coldest nights, in the darkest of days, and in the hardships that attempt to consume her. He speaks to her through His word and encourages her through tangible embraces of His love. Despite the seemingly endless seasons of suffering, He remains. The sun may rise and set at a different rhythm, and the tides will rise and fall at a new time, but His love is steadfast- and as the radiant expressions of fall twirl to the ground singling winter to come, His faithfulness prevails.

He prepares her heart each and every time. And while some days may seem lifeless and empty, she knew in the depth of her soul that He would never leave her nor forsake her because He illuminates past blessings to remind her of His presence when she cannot see any in her present.

Because she had survived the longest and most painful seasons, she could appreciate and prepare for the best of seasons. And because she knew how it felt to stand alone against the whipping winds of pain and discouragement, she could find ways to shield another who had yet to know a true spring. No matter what state of contentment or chaos she dwells in, He is with her, a guiding hand and luminescent light transforming the elements around her for His glory. So, she stands in any season and in any hardship and in any blessing, firm- because all of life is cradled in the arms of her Creator. He knows her by name and tells the sun when to rise and set. He speaks life into existence and pours blessings even into the rains. She trembles with fear and roars with His power as the storms above gather. There is no circumstance too great, no season too hard- for a God that made it all.

Over the years, her convictions and self-love had overshadowed any stain of trials in her life. She had too much self-respect to wallow in her misfortunes. She was strong because she had to be. Her only choice was to endure the pain that pushed her forward. Sometimes, being strong is the only option you've got, and she chose to be beautifully broken in the flames of her tragedies rather than just give up. She never asked why or felt ashamed of the struggles she'd survived, for the fires of her failures forged her iron spirit. She guarded her heart behind high walls and in deep places because she knew better than to risk heartache on undeserving issues.

It took only truly patient and compassionate hearts to see past the windows to her soul, willing to weather the storms of her fires to see the sparkle of her heart. She was no ordinary woman with a regular life; she was a reborn warrior with a heart of gold. She loved hard when there was love to be shared and chased her passions. She was too strong and too deep not to be. Regardless, she's a one-of-a-kind, oncein-a- lifetime lady, and she'll never settle for anything less than the best. No matter how her story unfolded, she'll always write it her way. Always unique, always strong and always beautifully free. No price too high, no journey too long, no obstacle too strong, no battle too fierce, no mountain too great, when your dream is the goal.

When you have a dream, do not let anything stop you. Your background shouldn't put your back on the ground, your weakness shouldn't stand in your way, what people say shouldn't make you sway, and several blows and hits shouldn't make you quit. Yes, there will be sacrifices to make and risky paths to take, but for every new day you are awake, commit to giving your dreams all it takes. If you give up on your dream, what's left? Dream, but when you rise, do something about it. Every step you take, no matter how small it is, counts in the big scheme of things. It's a great day, a great life, to go after what you see, no matter how you feel, push through to your dreams, and be true.

For one of the greatest joys in life is

to live the life of your dreams!

Life in service for Humanity!

www.ingramcontent.com/pod-product-compliance
Lightning Source LLC
Chambersburg PA
CBHW071105120626
46546CB00003B/1279